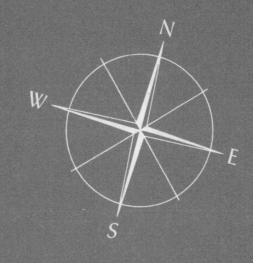

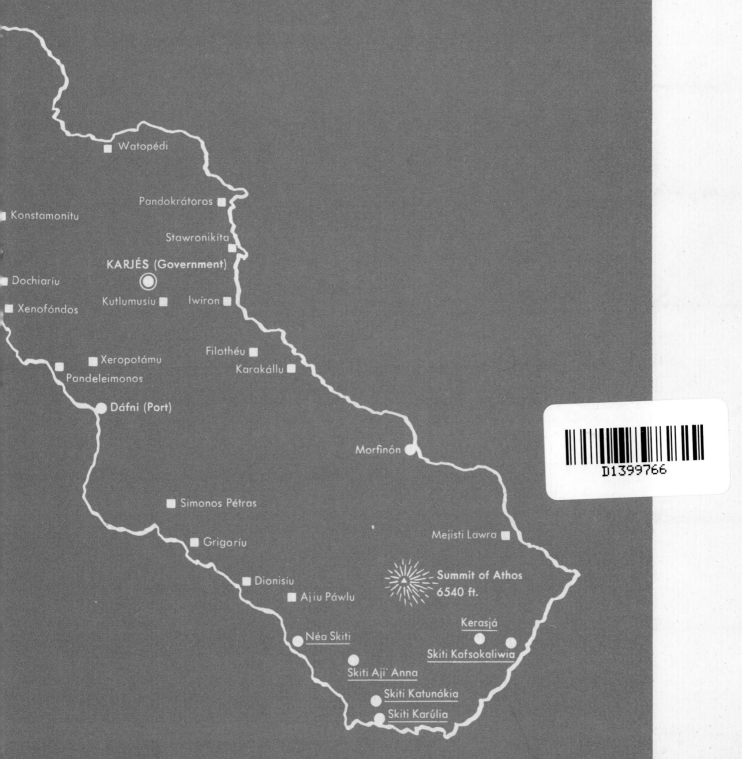

ATHOS

Dom Chrysostomus Dahm
Monk of the Abbey of Maria Laach

ATHOS

MOUNTAIN OF LIGHT

Text by Dom Chrysostomus Dahm

and Dom Ludger Bernhard

BURDA

Translated from the German by Aileen O'Brien

The authors' and translator's thanks are due to the Revd. A. M. Allchin, B. Litt. (Oxford),
Dr. J. N. Hillgarth (Cambridge) and Dr. O. K. Werkmeister (Berlin) for advice and assistance

TO THE REVEREND FATHERS

OF THE IERA KINOTIS

THE GOVERNMENT OF THE HOLY MOUNTAIN

ON THE OCCASION

OF THE THOUSANDTH ANNIVERSARY

OF ATHOS

IN RESPECT AND GRATITUDE

In search of a single descriptive phrase, succinct yet capable of embracing the whole of Mount Athos, that phenomenon of many facets, it is perhaps the phrase "spiritual preserve of Eastern Christianity" that first suggests itself for more reasons than one: here we find preserved the natural beauty of an enchanted island that, far from the turbulent world, unfolds inviolate before our wondering eyes. Here is preserved the almost static faith of the world of Byzantine Orthodoxy embodied in countless precious documents held safe behind the fortress-like walls of the great monasteries against the hungry maelstrom of a thousand years of history. Behind these same massive walls still burns the flame of early Christian monasticism with its uncompromising rejection of all the values the "world" holds expedient, its unquestioning, unconditional faith and a tenacious loyalty to the deep roots of its own tradition.

Off the beaten track of modern restlessness, aloof, created one might be tempted to say from the beginning of time to serve as refuge to honest seekers after God lies this island of peace, untouched by the two major wars of our time, tidal waves trailing cataclysmic consequences, that have swept in their wake the rest of the world.

Prolific in legends, shrouded in an aura of magic and mystery, smiled upon by a sky eternally blue, oblivious of the uneasy, storm-tossed, battling world about it, Athos is a fabulous dream peopled by disembodied souls. Even the steady stream of pilgrims that has always wended its way to Athos has dwindled in recent years to a mere trickle. They came either in search of absolution from the burden of their sins at the hands of the monks — the island's "saints" — or, in dire bodily or spiritual need, to implore the merciful protection of the "Panayía", for centuries beloved patroness of the island. Today it is almost exclusively scholars, writers, or globe-trotters with a taste for the unusual who trespass on the monks in their heavenly contemplation.

Lost in the mists of history are the names of the pious men who, in the earliest centuries of the Christian era, first felt the attraction of these lonely forests as a place where they could put into practice the harsh command of Christ to abandon father, mother, and brethren, and take the kingdom of God by storm, in fasting and in prayer. The irruption, almost exactly one thousand years ago, of St. Athanasius into their highly individual world of private devotion wherein each endeavoured to carry out his own conception of the ideal of personal sanctification, could not but appear to them an intolerable intrusion. Athanasius had come at the instance of his friend the Emperor Nikiphóros Phokás to found on soil already steeped in sanctity a community of monks who, living under a fixed rule of discipline and prayer, should join together in singing the praises of God. This first monastery became known as the Great Lávra and it served as a model for future foundations once the bitter opposition of the hermits was overcome.

The new order of things did not entail the disappearance of the eremitic form of life on Athos. It remains to this day a fastness wherein each man may carry out unhindered and according to his inclination his own ideal of personal piety, an attitude of tolerance admirably suited to the strongly individualistic Greek character. Among the twenty great monasteries on Athos there are those in which the ideal of the monks is a life of poverty and asceticism, under the rule of a permanent abbot, similar to that of the Western monastic orders. In other houses the monks live under the guidance of a body composed of a succession of elder monks. The brethren, each attended by a younger monk, remain independent and responsible for their individual households and their maintenance. The obligation of attendance at divine service is their only communal link. Each of these monasteries lives according to its own rule since religious orders, as we understand them in the West, exist neither on Athos nor elsewhere in the Eastern Church.

A third form of monastic life is that of the Skite, tiny communities of from three to four monks who, under the spiritual direction of an older monk, carry out their monastic duties while engaging in some form of manual labour. Occasionally a certain number of these communities unite to form a village. Lastly, there are those who choose, as others before them have done for over a thousand years, to be hermits and lead their own particular life of solitary devotion, some in caves high in the cliffs of the Holy Mountain, others as homeless wanderers roaming ceaselessly over the length and breadth of the peninsula.

Because of all this nowhere on earth could be made clearer to the reflective Western traveller the depth of the gulf that separates Eastern and Western thought, Eastern and Western piety. Everything in this hallowed spot, blessed alike by nature and by history, is steeped in a mystical symbolism. No object, no place, no act on Athos but is imbued, in the eyes of its monks, with a meaning far deeper than the mere outward semblance, and this not only in the sense of an ordinary parable — itself no more than a passing allegory born of the fanciful human intellect. The whole of their existence is impregnated with the Neo-platonic, in the last analysis Platonic, ontology they have inherited from the world of Late Antiquity.

To them the church is no mere house of prayer, a building whose walls and adornments reflect the fluctuating taste of centuries. Its outward design as well as the equipment and decoration of its interior are bodily symbols of a metaphysical reality, images, necessarily imperfect, of the Heavenly Jerusalem. The arching dome of the central cupola, rising from the richly frescoed circular walls of the drum is a symbol of Heaven itself and carries at its apex the stern image of the Judge of the World, a constant reminder to the onlooker of the ultimate realities. Within the confines of this limited space, symbol of limitless infinity, man himself becomes the necessarily imperfect likeness of one of those angels in the Heavenly Choirs who sing the praises of God in the Church Triumphant.

The figures of Our Lady and of the Saints depicted over and over again on every wall are to the monk not aesthetic decorations designed to create an atmosphere of spirituality. To him in each image is present, in a sense, the very person represented. The image is possessed of a share of his or her miraculous powers. Redolent of symbolism are likewise each liturgical vestment, each sacred vessel, even the mighty corona or wheel-like candelabra that hangs before the iconostasis, while the very swaying of the corona has its meaning.

Food, the unavoidable means of preserving a physical life itself essential to uninterrupted praise of God, is hallowed, and thus becomes a religious ceremony as does every unavoidable function of daily existence. The walls of the Trápeza where meals are partaken to the accompaniment of prayer and pious reading are just as rich in images of Saints and Virtues as the walls of the church itself. This all-pervading "Weltanschauung" that floods the whole of his life with a mystical radiance undoubtedly accounts for the fact that in the monk's eyes everything partakes of the miraculous and that there is hardly a solitary tree, hardly a spring or a cliff of unusual outline round which his imagination does not instinctively weave some marvellous legend.

Clearly, an understanding of the monks and their life will be vouchsafed only to the traveller who, eschewing haste and idle curiosity, approaches the island free of prejudice or arrogance and who, armed with knowledge of the historical past from which their attitude springs, is prepared to linger, unhurried and with open mind, in their monasteries. His first acquaintance with their world of mysticism will be made at the narrow borderland where even the angelic community of Athos is tied down to earth and cannot avoid making contact with the world of sin. The social obligations arising out of this contact are fulfilled by the monks with tact and polished grace. The stranger is welcomed with every outward sign of the unfeigned hospitality to be found all over Greece. Everything that sea, garden or cellar can offer is his to command, with no obligation on his side of sharing the rigidly self-denying fasts practised by the community. His own bed is a relatively comfortable one but rarely, if ever, will he be afforded a glimpse of a monastic cell and thereby the opportunity of comparing the softness of his own couch with the hardness of the bed on which the monk, even during the short hours of the night, carries on his unrelenting conflict with the Devil. On the other hand he may, but only if he chooses, rise at three or four o'clock in the morning to the rhythmic beat of the hammer on the Símandron in the monastery courtyard and join the monks in their never ending chanting of the psalms.

It would be an error to suppose that these brethren, who acknowledge only the "True Philosophy" — the Apathía — are addicted to scholarly pursuits. In the sight of eyes unwaveringly focussed on another world, even learning is tainted with presumption when not with sinful curiosity. Their libraries are stocked with literature which is mainly spiritual and edifying, the manuscript works of the Fathers of the early Middle Ages, and those champions of a later period who, from the stronghold of Athos led the battle of Eastern Orthodoxy against the tenets of Rome.

The archives of Athos, unlike others within the former frontiers of Byzantium, are relatively rich in chrysobulls testifying to the princely gifts and grants of land received from Byzantine Emperors and other Orthodox rulers. This curious circumstance is explained by the fact that Athos was left relatively undisturbed by the Sultans of Turkey but it is also due to the special measures taken for the documents' preservation by the monks acting on a belief deep-rooted on the Holy Mountain: that Constantine XII Paleológos, last Emperor of Byzantium, who fell on the ramparts of Constantinople in the year 1453 while defending his doomed Empire against the Turks, will one day rise from his secret grave, replant the banner of the Cross upon Ayía Sophía, and inaugurate for the monasteries of Athos a new age of splendour reminiscent of the ancient days of glory.

It would be a vain hope to suppose that the Holy Mountain can entirely escape the threat of secularisation that tends everywhere to engulf all things holy and sacred. The voices clamouring that the ancient privileges of the Holy Mountain be broken down and the splendid beauty of Athos turned to profit grow ever louder. We can only trust that the Orthodox Faith of the East will stand firm in its refusal to deliver up to the "world" this place unique on earth, devoted solely to the exercise of a truly profound piety and where a nearness to God is felt by every visitor who sets foot on its holy soil.

Dr. Franz Dölger
Professor at the University of Munich.

Introduction

In the course of three trips to Mount Athos, we were there a total of four months, we took some seven thousand photographs of which one hundred and sixty have been chosen to illustrate this book.

The book begins by showing the land both as a whole, and in certain typical details. We then take the road to Karyés, seat of the government of the Monks' Republic, with its house of Parliament, the Protáton, or church, and the monasteries inhabited by the members of the government. Chapter three deals with the Great Lávra, first of the monasteries to be founded by St. Athanasios in the tenth century, with its church, the famous refectory, various treasures and the tomb of the founder. Next comes Vatopédi, second in order of foundation, which had the distinction of erecting the first academy of learning on Athos, spiritual forbear of the recently opened School of Athos.

It was in the ruling monasteries that the monks first lived as a community but later, in the sixteenth century, a movement of reformation created the Skíte or village type of community to which many monks retired from the large monasteries. Most of the icon painters live today in Skíte.

Next comes the Katholikón, or main church, with its numberless icons. It is the scene of innumerable religious ceremonies that come to a climax at the feast of the Resurrection, Easter, of imposing magnificence.

The book closes with a view of the Holy Mountain itself, symbol of the transfiguration through fasting and prayer that is the goal of every monk who lives out his life at its foot.

Maria Laach, August 6, 1959

Feast of the Transfiguration of Our Lord.

Dom Chrysostomus Dahm

A Green Land, Cliffs and the Sea

For days before our departure from Salonica, en route for Athos, it had rained. Lakes had formed in the depressions of the road that leads, over hills and down dales, to Ierissós. Small streams, harmless usually, had grown to raging torrents that constantly threatened the safety of our overcrowded motor coach. The aged vehicle creaked and groaned in such alarming fashion that the passengers kept on glancing at each other apprehensively, obviously fearing the worst. However, with nothing more serious than a delay of one hour we arrived at Ierissós toward four o'clock in the afternoon. We had taken eight hours to drive ninety miles.

At Ierissós we discovered that it would be impossible to sail for Dáphni, our port of disembarkation on Athos, that night. This was a keen disappointment, as for months we had been looking forward to setting foot on the legendary shores of the world of monks. We had spent hours and days dreaming of it, discussing it, and wondering about it. A group of our fellow travellers, Greek merchants whose object was the purchase of timber, oil, and nuts from the monasteries on the peninsula, set about finding a boatman who might be induced to make a special trip. After considerable wangling and haggling one boatman declared himself willing to make the crossing to the monastery of Ivíron for the sum of three hundred drachmas. We promptly joined the party, delighted after all to be able to reach our goal on the day we had planned and to sleep under a monastery roof.

The sun had begun its rapid descent towards the horizon as we boarded our ship at five o'clock. The fields round Ierissós had taken on their autumnal look as of scorched steppes. Gone were all the gay colours of spring and summer, gone was the red splash of geraniums in window-boxes and the bright gardens. A late October mist crept stealthily over the flat, parched land.

We could not have been more than half a mile out when, from behind a jutting headland, and rising straight out of the sea, there appeared the "Ayion Oros", the Holy Mountain itself, towering in unparalleled majesty over the gigantic granite block of Athos. A sudden wind, sprung up in the east, checked the progress of our ship as if with a restraining hand. It howled overhead and seemed to drag at our frail, struggling little craft, tossing us on high only to fling us back into the trough of the next wave. Shivering, we climbed into our wind jackets and crawled lower into the boat, our gaze fixed on the land that, despite the storm, grew steadily nearer. Already the wind was laden with heady smells of exotic plants, shrubs and herbs. The graying day rapidly sank into night. A paraffin lamp was hoisted to our mast and threw a cone shaped stream of light over the heaving seas. Occasionally we sailed so close to shore that shadowy cliffs peered down at us out of the night, and once the high silhouette of a monastery glided past, etched against the dark night sky. Fishermen were busy along the shore, preparing to set out to sea, the brilliant lights they use to attract the fish already burning at the stern of their boats. We could hear the rattle of anchor chains and the hissing of lamps intermingling with the sound of voices that occasionally hailed us from the shore.

It was only eight o'clock when we landed at Iviron, but from the quiet that surrounded us it might have been midnight. No footstep sounded, no window showed a light. The land of monks slept as we set foot, in silence and filled with awe, on the sacred soil of Athos where for a thousand years saints, monks, and hermits without number had lived and died.

An immense oaken door surmounted by an arched gallery loomed out of the darkness. We knocked and waited, then went on knocking. After what seemed an age we heard footsteps within. The door opened slowly and the black figure of a monk became visible in a slit of light. Our Greek friends briefly explained our predicament and we were admitted. We crossed the wide monastery courtyard and were shown into a room with a long table spread with a white cloth. After the darkness outside, the light from a paraffin lamp seemed blinding. The Guest Master, who appeared not to mind being roused out of his sleep, greeted us with a cheerfulness obviously and reassuringly sincere. While he saw to it that a hot meal was prepared for us a younger monk made up our beds. Overcome by the warmth of the hospitality we soon sank gratefully into sleep.

Our first glimpse of Athos, next morning, was unforgettable. After a night loud with storm and rain the day broke cloudless and calm. The glistening early sun shone through ethereal veils of mist that draped the tree clad cliffs and hung over the sea, clothing roofs, gardens and fields, in a cloak of shimmering crystals. The land of monks, resplendent in its rich autumnal colours looked like a garden of paradise.

The Guest Master brought us hot tea and bread and gave us to understand that we must travel that very morning to Karyés, the capital of the Monastic Republic, and obtain the Athos "passport" without which travellers are not normally admitted to any of the monasteries on the peninsula.

In the cool of the morning, we set off. At first the road led through groves of olive trees so old as to seem primeval. The air was heady with the smell of herbs, plants and fading flowers, all of which were strange to us. Soon it became difficult to keep to the road. Rotting tree trunks had fallen across it and torrents like waterfalls engulfed it, in places forcing us to abandon it and scramble straight up the mountain slope as best we could. Half way up monastic cells began to appear, often overgrown with luxuriant greenery. Some of them lay deserted and we learned that the number of those who were willing to replace a monk when he died and embrace the solitude that had been his, grew steadily less.

Time and again we were made to wonder at the practical sense allied to an exquisite feeling for natural beauty that guided the monks in their choice of sites for their buildings. From one of the high terraces, the view on one side swept over the endless spreading sea, over plunging cliffs, luxuriant green slopes and hills studded with cypresses. On the other it soared to the very top of the Holy Mountain, rising before our eyes like a ceaseless admonition to fasting and to prayer.

That was on our first trip. Eighteen months later we found ourselves once more on the soil of Athos. The Monastic Government had invited us to return in connection with the preparations for the thousandth anniversary of its foundation. This time we avoided the bus ride to Ierissós by sailing direct, one warm May night, from Salonica to Dáphni, the only official port on Athos, aboard the freighter "Ayíos Nikolaos". Above, a brilliant, infinite mosaic made up of a myriad stars filled the dome of the sky. The silence of the night was broken only by the steady beat of the ship's engine.

The following afternoon, towards three o'clock, the "Ayíos Nikolaos" neared the peninsula. We sat on deck in the midst of packing cases and all the ship's gear. Round us sprawled young Greeks in ragged trousers and sweaty shirts, most of them barefoot, come to Athos in search of work at the monasteries. On our right, the mighty peak of the Holy Mountain emerged gradually from the enveloping mists. The monasteries of Grigoríou, Dionysíou and Simópetra stood out vividly against a background of stark cliffs or soft green hillsides. On our left, like a great fortress, rose the Russian monastery of St. Pandeleímon, built by the Tzars a century ago to house two thousand monks.

Our ship made straight as an arrow for Dáphni. The roofs and walls of the town's few houses were brilliant splashes of red and white in the sun. Towards five o'clock we dropped anchor opposite the pier and young workmen from the port rowed us ashore. A government messenger from Karyés awaited us with the news that mules for the transport of our mountain of luggage would not be available until the next day. We were to spend the night at the monastery of Xeropotámou, overlooking the port. Leaving our baggage in the care of a merchant who offered to keep it for us locked in a warehouse overnight, we made our way to the monastery whose hospitable portal we reached before the sun had set.

ὁωαρη τὰ νοήματα αὐ
μῶν ἀ̓πὸ τῆς ἁπλό
τητος τῆς εἰς τὸν χν̅
μὲν γὰρ ὁ ἐρχόμενος
ἀλ̅ον ι̅ν̅ κηρύσσει·
ὁν ὁυκ εκηρύξαμε(ν)
η̅ πν̅α ετερον λαμβάνε
ται· ὁ ὁυκ ελάβεται·
ἡ εὐαγγέλιον ετερον
ὁ ὁυκ εδεξασθαι,
καλῶς αν· εἴχεσθαι·
λογίζομαι γὰρ μηδὲν
ὑστερηκέναι τῶ(ν)
ὑπερ λίαν ἀ̓ποστόλω(ν)
ει δε και ἱδιωτη τησ ελογω
αλλ̅ ου τη γνωσει

Karyés, the Seat of Government

The deeper we penetrated into this land of monks and the more we learned of their lives the clearer it became to us how utterly different from ours is the structure of their monasticism. They acknowledge no duty towards mankind in the way of practical pastoral work. Further still, they deliberately turn their backs on the world and on any collaboration with it in any form whatsoever. This absolute denial of every form of activity — even in parochial or cultural fields — may appear senseless to the Western mind, yet it is precisely this apparent passivity that gives to Eastern monasticism its distinctive and valuable character. On Athos the traveller comes face to face with an age old fascinating concept of monastic life that, ever since the days of St. Anthony of Egypt, has seemed the only logical one to men whose sole aim is union with God and who, in order to achieve it, have taken Him, quite simply, at His word: "Give up the world and follow me."

Our meeting with the Fathers at Karyés the next afternoon served to confirm us in our original opinion. The Protespistátis, surrounded by his Epistáte, or ministers, received us with great kindness at the Government building. After an exchange of greetings we were shown into the reception room where we sat with the Fathers. A young monk clad in the ráson, a flowing, ceremonial gown, tended us a silver tray of glycó, the drink with which the traveller is welcomed to every Athos monastery. To the accompaniment of obeisances in the direction of the Fathers we partook of dried, candied figs, a glass of water, a glass of ouzo — a spicy liqueur flavoured with anis — and lastly of tiny cups of Turkish coffee. This ceremony was followed by another of the first importance to any foreigner on Athos: the handing over, by the Secretary of the Government, of the diamonitírion, or passport that grants the traveller permission to remain on Athos for a determined period and the right to be received at all its monasteries. Father Andreas handed us our passports and wished us a very happy stay on the Holy Mountain. Our interview with the Fathers had lasted two hours because we were able to converse with them in Greek, but, to us it had gone like a flash. In the meantime, Father Aléxandros, who acted as Secretary for Home Affairs, had arranged for our accommodation at the adjacent monastery of Koutloumousíou. Taking leave of our kind hosts we stepped out on to the broad flight of steps that leads down from the Government building to the square. The last rays of the sun slanted over Karyés, washing monasteries and alleyways, the market square and the Protáton that stood directly opposite us, in an indescribably mellow light. To the south, against a cloudless sky, dominating as always, the peak of the Holy Mountain turned slowly to the colour of rose.

The market square lay deserted. From the quiet that reigned everywhere we concluded that the monks had already retired for the night.

Night services often begin in the dark monastery churches before midnight and the main portal of all monasteries closes at sundown. The windows of every cell were closely shuttered. The only sound was a trickle of voices from the tavern patronised by muleteers and workmen.

At our feet rose the Protáton, a basilica-like church almost ten centuries old. How much history had its ancient stones survived! Out of the silence, our imagination conjured up scene after scene of the long, involved and turbulent drama that had been played out on this market place, silent witness to a chapter in the story of Christendom second to none in significance and importance.

In the tenth century, monks, who up to then had lived scattered all over the peninsula, decided to meet and to elect a Superior from among their number, who, as Prótos, and with the support of a Sýnaxis or Council of Elders, should sit in Karyés and there deal with the problems of the community as a whole. Some years later the Prótos and his Council erected a church which they called the Protáton, and a series of monastic dwellings for their helpers. The frescoes that cover the Protáton's walls were painted in the fourteenth century by a celebrated artist from Salonica, Pansélinos. They have recently been renovated and the original brilliance of their colours restored, on the initiative of the representative of the Greek Government on Athos, Governor Konstantópoulos. The centuries that followed the erection of the Protáton saw the building of countless churches and chapels all over the peninsula, and their interiors were adorned by painters officially appointed to do so. Monasteries, cells, and hermitages followed and finally, the Konákia, residence of the members of the Monastic Parliament and Government.

The Ierá Kinótis or Holy Synod of today is merely the modern development of the original Sýnaxis and its head is the Protepistátis, successor of the Prótos. The Monastic Parliament is composed of twenty elected representatives of the ruling monasteries, called Andiprósopi. From their number four Epistáte are elected annually and compose the Epistasía, a sort of higher executive body of which the Protepistátis, or Prótos, is the head. One of the functions of the Epistasía is the wielding of the official seal by virtue of which certain documents, such as the Athos passport, for example, become valid. Each of the four Epistáte has in his possession and care one quarter of the seal. The full validity of a document comes from the application to it of all four quarters of the seal. Lately, however, the number of visitors to Athos has increased to such an extent that the old cumbersome system of individually applying each quarter of the seal has had to be abandoned in the case of passports. An ordinary rubber stamp — whereon the lines of the former divisions are still clearly marked — has replaced the old seal. In the case of important decisions the agreement of each of the four Epistáte is still required.

The delegates of the ruling monasteries meet at regular intervals, like any other Parliament, and during their long sessions they discuss questions tabled by the Government itself or by any of the delegates. Subsequent visits to Karyés afforded us interesting sidelights on the kind of question that Parliament discusses and the Epistáte decide on: for instance the granting of increased funds for the building of roads or the upkeep of monasteries and churches, the appointment of teachers to the School of Athos, invitations to be issued to important foreign guests and countless legal questions involving monks and laymen alike. We happened to be at Karyés on one occasion when a monk and a lay employee had been arraigned before Parliament to account for an unauthorized money transaction.

For the opening of a session of Parliament each of the four Epistáte is called upon at his dwelling by a Polilarches — a civilian employee — and ceremoniously conducted across the market square and up the broad steps into the Hall of Parliament. While witnessing this ceremony we reflected on the endless stream of men that had drifted across the market place in the course of a thousand years: monks, hermits, abbots, high dignitaries of every land, even Turks representing the great Sultans of Islam, processions, hosts and hosts of pilgrims. And in our own day, German and Greek soldiers, tourists, men of all nations and classes, of all beliefs or of none. Now we, sons of St. Benedict, monks of the West, stood here in admiration before the monks of the East. Our growing acquaintance with the Protáton and the monasteries, our gradually acquired knowledge of the difficult history of the generations of monks that had lived here, stirred in our hearts a longing for a day we hoped not far distant when monks of East and West should meet, no longer as strangers but as brothers should, who are moved by a common aim: by means of a life of fasting, unremitting prayer and striving towards God, to gain for themselves and for the whole world the light of eternal life.

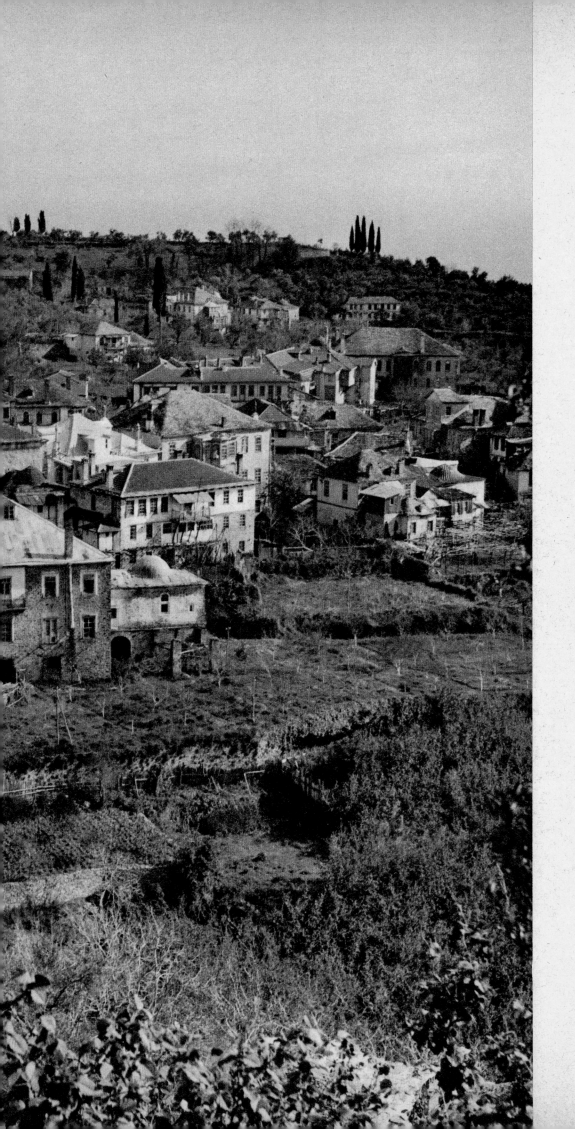

ΙΕΡΑ ΕΠΙCΤΑCΙΑ
ΑΓΙΟΥ ΟΡΟΥC
ΑΘΩ
—

Αριθ. Πρωτ. 152/Δ.

Καρυαι τη 4η Μαΐου 1957

Π ρ ο ς

Τας Εικοσιν Ιερας και Σεβασμιας ημων Μονας
του Αγιου Ορους Αθω.

        Οι επιφεροντες το παρον συστατηριον ημων γραμμα
λιαν ευσεβεις, φιλελληνες και φιλοι του Αγιωνυμου ημων Τοπου,
PER. PERE. LOUDGER BERNHARD , Καθηγητης εν Μοναχῳ των Ανα-
τολικων γλωσσων, και CHRYSOSTOMUS D A H M, P. Καλλιτεχνης
Φωτογραφος, ετυχον επισημου ειδικης αδειας εξ αποφασεως της
καθ'ημας Ιερας Κοινοτητος, υπο στοιχειον ΙΕ/15-3-57, μετακλη-
θεντες υπο των ενταυθα Αρχων δια την ληψιν καλλιτεχνικων φωτο
γραφιων εκ των καλυτερων Βυζαντινων και μεταβυζαντινων μνημει-
ων τεχνης και αντικειμενων (εικονες-μινιατουρες κλπ.)προς εκ-
τυπωσιν βιβλιων περι Αγιου Ορους και βελτιωσιν των ενθυμιων
(αλμπουμ) επισκεπτων Αγιου Ορους.
        Συνιστωντες οθεν Αυτους τη Υμετερα αγαπητη ημιν
Πανοσιολογιοτητι, ολως ιδιαιτερως, παρακαλουμεν αδελφικως οπως
παρασχεθη Αυτοις η προσηκουσα διευκολυνσις και αδεια Υμων δια
το εργον των καθως και η εγνωσμενη πατροπαραδοτος φιλοξενια.-

            Λ ι α ν   φ ι λ α δ ε λ φ ω ς

Οι Επισταται της Ιερας Κοινοτητος του Αγιου Ορους Αθω

Ο Βατοπαιδιου   Πρωτεπιστατης Περ. Μπαλεντινος

" Κουτλουμουσιου Επιστατης Περ. Σωφρονιος

" Καρακαλλου   "   Γ. Βασχω

" Σταυρονικητα   α.α. Γ. Ιωακειμ Σκωτοπεγοια

The Lávra, First of the Ruling Monasteries

The silence, serenity and peace that had reigned undisturbed until then were shattered when, in the year 963, the south eastern point of Athos echoed to the noise and bustle of building operations.

On a gentle slope at the spot where the Holy Mountain rises in one swift, majestic thrust, but far enough from the sea to be safe from the spray of waves lashed to fury in a storm, lay the foundations of a building of dimensions undreamed of till then on Athos. It was all the more surprising since, one hundred years previously, the peninsula had been reserved by Imperial decree for the exclusive use of pious hermits and those of like mind who had inhabited Athos for centuries past.

The new foundation grew into a vast, irregular, lengthy rectangle of massive walls capable of encompassing not only the living and working quarters already planned but further buildings on an equally large scale. Amongst these must be mentioned first of all the Katholikón, or main church, where the monks assemble for the celebration of religious services. Directly before the church, where the vestibule of the main entrance stands, is the phiáli, or holy water font. At the beginning of every month, and during a solemn ceremony on the Feast of the Epiphany — the commemoration of the Baptism of Christ — water is blessed in the great stone bowl under a canopy supported on pillars.

In a direct line running from the main portal to the church through the phiáli is the entrance to the celebrated Trápeza, or refectory. The monks look on the food of the body as a symbol of the food of the soul taken during the sacrifice of the Mass. On certain feast days, therefore, a procession made up of priests and lay monks, the former in liturgical vestments, the latter in their choir robes, preceded by lighted candles and to the accompaniment of chants and prayers, proceeds solemnly from the church to the refectory where all partake of food.

The fact that the monastery was planned to house a closed community is obvious. The towering walls that surround the whole were not built primarily as a protection against enemies bent on destruction and plunder, but as a symbol and an expression of monastic community life. And it was precisely to this communal system of life that the tenth century Athos monks objected. From time immemorial they had lived in lonely hermitages, hidden caves, or loosely knit communities of huts so primitive as hardly to afford protection against the weather. There they had practised unremitting self denial, fasts and penances, each according to his taste, under the direction of a master, certainly, but one that each monk had chosen freely for himself. To such as these, life behind rigid stone walls, according to a rule no less rigid that, not content with dictating their religious exercises, regulated their sleeping and eating habits as well, was all but inconceivable. Worst of all, the rule, for all its inflexibility, had been whittled down to the spiritual stature of the average member of a community, and thus, in the eyes of the monks, was a step backward along the road of perfect monastic self denial. They also feared that strict monastic discipline would limit the freedom of their spiritual life, hitherto absolute. It went hard with them to accept all this in silence but they were in no position to offer any practical opposition to the project.

The founder of the new form of monasticism was St. Athanásios, a close personal friend and favourite of Nikiphóros Phokás, recently crowned Emperor at Constantinople. The two had met when Nikiphóros Phokás was a general in command of troops and Athanásios, who came of a wealthy family of Trebizond, had entered a monastery in Asia Minor. Athanásios subsequently left his monastery and came to Athos where, with the approval and the financial support of the Emperor, he founded the Great Lávra. It was the Emperor's intention one day to abdicate his throne, retire to Athos and, living there as a monk, strive after perfection under the spiritual guidance of his friend. Before the Emperor could realize his plan to renounce the glories of this world he was murdered by his nephew John I Tsimiskis, adulterous lover of the Empress Theóphano.

The monks, still loyal to the old eremitical ideal, decided to strike for freedom. They dispatched a delegation to Constantinople requesting that all Athanásios' rules he abolished and his work set at naught. The new Emperor, spurred on perhaps by a guilty conscience or more likely out of fear of the spiritual power wielded by his murdered predecessor's saintly friend, sent back a new constitution affecting the whole of the monastic population of the peninsula. In it the position of preponderance of the new foundation, to be called the Great Lávra, was made quite clear. Further, as a physical expression of his determination to support St. Athanásios, the Emperor caused the walls of the Lávra to be strengthened and he built the great keep which dominates the whole and which to this day is called the "Tower of Tsimiskis".

Tsimiskis and his wife Theodora showered the Lávra with gifts of gold and silver, precious stones and costly brocades. During the centuries that followed and for as long as Emperors of Byzantium ruled at Constantinople, its riches continued to increase. In spite of the decline that set in with the Turkish domination and a considerable amount of sporadic plundering by sea pirates and others, the Lávra still possesses important manuscripts in costly bindings, gold-embroidered silken vestments and liturgical vessels of gold and silver set with precious stones.

It is extraordinary how what is called the "genius loci", the deep rooted, fundamental idea that is the very essence of a place tends periodically to come back to life, however deeply it may be buried. The Lávra was built by St. Athanásios in the teeth of bitter opposition from monks long established on the peninsula who, out of unreasoning but unswerving loyalty to the old eremitical ideal closed their hearts to the new order and who, had they found a way of avoiding it, would never have suffered its presence on "their" Athos. Some centuries later it was precisely in the Lávra that the new idiorhythmic idea found an enthusiastic reception. The principle underlying the idiorhythmic rule is that while still belonging to the community, each monk remains his own master in spiritual things and master as well of his own private fortune. The monastery is no longer ruled by an abbot elected for life but by a group of representatives freely chosen from among the brethren and elected for a term of one year. Of these one enjoys precedence over the rest but only as a "primus inter pares" and the government of the house is carried out along democratic principles.

Community life is restricted to attendance in common of religious services. Otherwise each monk lives, cooks and eats alone, or in groups of two or three, exactly as in the old eremitical days. As a consequence, the beautifully ornamented Trápeza, the great refectory, has sunk to the level of a museum that can be shown to visitors at any time.

The Trápeza is a long building, built rather like a church, on a cruciform foundation. In an apse there is a raised platform for the superiors of the monastery. The walls are covered with frescoes painted in 1512 by an artist of the Cretan school. At the entrance the Last Judgement is represented while in the central nave there are three superimposed tiers of saints with scenes from their lives and their martyrdoms and lastly, the saints in their heavenly glory. This splendid hall, radiant with the beauty and colour of its frescoes, is put to its original use only three times a year when the monks assemble and partake of a meal in common.

The monks of the Meyísti Lávra, which guards within its walls the grave of the founder of the first cenobitic monastery on Mount Athos, today live out their lives in an individualistic isolation of their own choosing.

57   General view of the Great Lávra, looking east.

58   Plan of the monastery buildings. (Archondaríkion, or Guesthouse. Epitropía or administrative offices. Katholikón, or main church. Trápeza, or refectory.)

59   View from the watchtower, looking east. (See plan.)

60   St. Athanásios, founder of the Lávra. A painting on parchment.

61   Interior of the church with iconostasis, corona and candelabra.

62   View of the Katholikón and its cupolas.

63   Procession of icons preceded by singers.

64   Cover of a Book of the Gospels representing Christ in a standing position, in the Byzantine tradition.

65   Ancient T-shaped abbot's staff with enamel work and precious stones, from the church treasure.

66   Father Ambrósios, for years the beloved prior of the Great Lávra.

67   The richly frescoed entrance to the Trápeza and a cypress that is a thousand years old.

68   The unique interior of the Trápeza with its sixteenth century frescoes.

70   Majestic paintings cover the Trápeza from floor to ceiling.

71   An old monk meditates in the sun before the Trápeza.

72   Tomb of St. Athanásios, founder of the Great Lávra, a place of pilgrimage for all the monks on Athos.

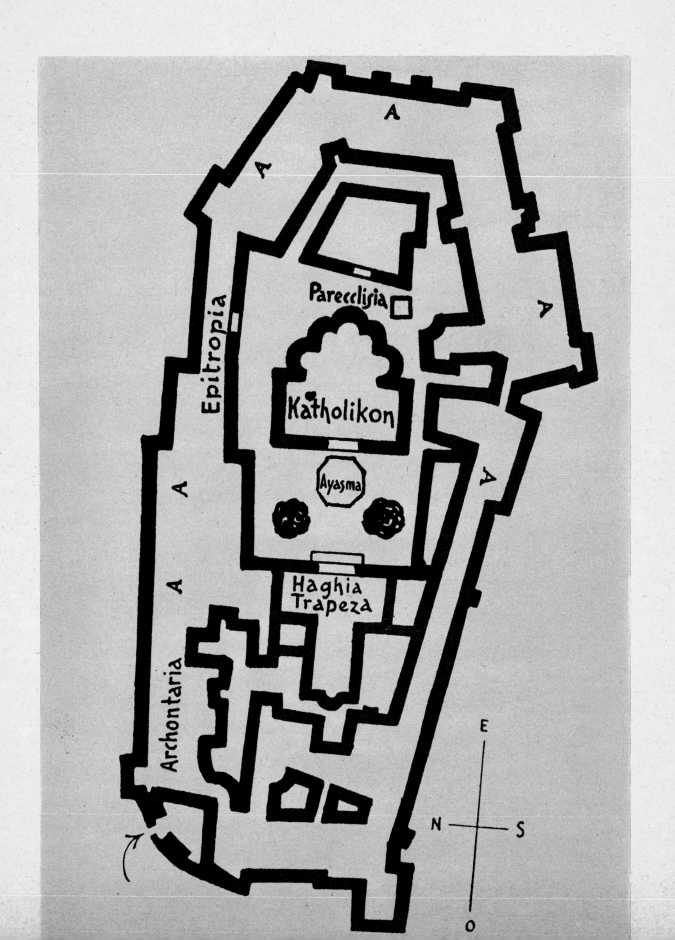

A
A
A
Parecclisia
Epitropia
Katholikon
Ayasma
A
A
Haghia
Trapeza
A
Archontaria

E
N — S
O

Ο ΑΓ ΠΡ
Ο
ΟС

†ΑΤΤΑΡ
ΝΗСΑ
ΜΕΝΟΙ
ΠΑΝΤΑ
ΤΕΡΠΝΑΚ
ΕΠΙΚΑΡΑ
ΤΠΑΝ
ΤΕΙС

60

Vatopédi, the Academy and the new School of Athos

The main front of the monastery of Vatopédi is enriched with a remarkable decoration of brickwork. The most striking of these ornaments, visible at a considerable distance, is the "Yin-Yang" sign, Chinese symbol of the mutual interaction of the static and active in all things. To us this seemed to indicate that the monks of Vatopédi were the least affected by the narrowness of mind inevitable in an existence deliberately restricted to a limited monastic world and that they had remained to an astonishing degree receptive to modern thought and development. Further proof of this seemed the installation of an electric light system fed by a generator which — also typically — has not worked for years although the intention of having it repaired "soon" remains as firm as ever.

A modern mechanical clock tells the time at Vatopédi while other monasteries go by the ancient Byzantine system that, depending on the time of year and their special importance, divides holy days and nights each into twelve "hours" of varying length. Vatopédi has even gone so far as to adopt the Gregorian calendar, while all the other monasteries have remained faithful to the ancient Julian calendar and in consequence lag thirteen days behind the rest of the civilized world.

It would seem that a progressive spirit is traditional at Vatopédi. It can hardly be chance that decided the Patriarch Cyril V in 1743, to build in conjunction with Melétios, archpriest of Vatopédi, the so-called "Athos Academy" on a hill overlooking the monastery. The underlying purpose of the foundation was to help raise the level of education and culture, that, throughout the former Byzantine Empire, had sunk extremely low under the yoke of Turkish domination. The academy was not designed exclusively nor even primarily for the education of the monks of Athos. Indeed, when Ewyénios Voúlgaris, celebrated as one of the most learned men of his age, was named director of the school in 1753 it was attended by students from every corner of the Orthodox world. The policy of the new Rector, who had received his education in the universities of Europe, was to join together the wisdom of classical antiquity, modern learning, and the philosophy of the Enlightenment, and to place the whole at the service of theology.

The monks of Athos, however, viewed this invasion of the Holy Mountain by profane science as a mortal danger to the very reason of their existence on the island and incompatible with the spirit of asceticism that shuns every contact with the things of this world. A campaign against the school and its head was soon under way and accusations of dangerous innovations in the teaching of matters pertaining to the Faith reached the Patriarch. In the end Voúlgaris, defeated, voluntarily resigned his post and left Athos forever, thus sealing the fate of the Academy. Abandoned by its students, it was closed by an official decree of the Patriarch in 1759.

After the closing of the Academy silence settled once again over Vatopédi, nestling on the gentle slopes above the bay, like a minute walled city out of the Italian Middle Ages. Prosperous times brought an increase in wealth and in the number of monks with a consequent expansion of the outer walls and the living and working quarters they enclose. The monastery enclosure, as it stands today, has the aspect of a series of wide, slowly ascending steps on which churches and chapels, fountains and shrines, the Trápeza, the bell tower and other buildings stand. It gives the impression of spaciousness and suggests that here it is possible to hold at bay narrowness of mind and every cramping limitation to the questing spirit.

Almost exactly one hundred years after the foundation of the ill-fated Academy, in the year 1842 a second school was established on Athos by the monks themselves and for their own private use. It was not to be a university but more a Theological Seminary, or high school, destined to give certain chosen candidates an education sufficient to enable them to fill secretarial and other posts in the monasteries and in the Monastic Government.

In 1930 this establishment was replaced by a theological school that retained the character of a secondary, or high school, as well. It was run officially by the Ierá Kinótis but its obvious intention of raising the general level of culture on the peninsula did not meet with the approval of all the monks. It was closed during the Second World War.

In 1953 the more progressive elements on Athos, with the collaboration and aid of the Greek Government, founded on an entirely new basis the "Athoniás Ekklisiastikí Scholí". The "Athonite Church School" possesses, in the person of Bishop Nathanaíl, a director who not only has studied at the universities of Greece and of Western Europe, but is also a monk of the Great Lávra. This fortunate circumstance may well serve to widen the horizon of the younger monks of Athos.

The new school is housed in a wing of the Russian monastery of St. Andrew, which belongs to Vatopédi. The Greek Government officially recognizes the school and its examinations. It also appoints and pays the teaching staff. Subjects of an exclusively monastic or religious character are taught by qualified monks. All others are entrusted to laymen with the usual diplomas. The student body is not restricted to monks of the various monasteries on Athos but includes boys and youths who have not yet taken final vows but whose intention nevertheless is eventually to join one of the monasteries. In 1957 the number of students was fifty, of whom eighteen were professed monks. The full course lasts for six years and comprises, for its younger pupils, an ordinary school curriculum, but for the older students courses and subjects that belong in fact to the domain of theology.

Plans to turn the existing establishment into a full fledged high school developing into a theological seminary are being put into operation step by step. How will a new departure such as this fare in the hermetically sealed society of Athos, traditionally hostile to education and to science? Will the graduates of the new school experience exclusion and distrust at the hands of those of their brethren who hold with only the most rudimentary form of education?

In any event it is certain that both time and a new generation of men will be needed to break down completely the aversion to "useless knowledge" so deep rooted in the monks of Athos. Moreover, it will be necessary to prove in practice that monasticism and education are not incompatible, but capable of yielding a deeper meaning and bringing richer fruits each to the other.

Whoever has seen these students, in the flower of their youth, at work under the guidance of ideally disposed teachers cannot doubt that this is the soil from which the thousand year old monasticism of Athos may yet gain new strength.

77   The main entrance to Vatopédi in the morning sunlight.

78   Ruins of the eighteenth century aqueduct of the Academy above Vatópedi.

79   Father Theóphilos, an eminent and progressive monk of Vatopédi.

80   General view of Vatopédi from the site of the old Academy.

82   Bishop Nathanaíl, Rector of the new school at Karyés, a monk of the Great Lávra.

83   Entrance to the new school in the monastery of St. Andrew.

84   The Russian monastery of St. Andrew, that belongs to Vatopédi.

86   Father Nikódimos, teacher of Byzantine chant.

87   Students and teachers in the school courtyard during recess.

88   The youngest class conducted by a teacher from Athens.

89   Ambrósios, a student monk from the Lávra and secretary to the Bishop.

90   Monks and students set the tables for guests of the government.

91   A student and novice from the monastery of the Pandokrátoros.

92   The youngest member of the school: fourteen year old Dimítrios of Karakállou.

The Twenty Ruling Monasteries

Undoubtedly, the conception of Athos as being primarily a land of hermits, has always been deep rooted on the island, but in the tenth century the practical development of monasticism tended towards life in enclosed communities. In any event, historical sources show that two further large monasteries were built almost simultaneously with the Lávra: Vatopédi, with which we dealt in the last chapter, and Ivíron, the "Monastery of the Iberians". The Iberians, or Georgians, were a people who had been converted to Christianity at an early date and who, living in the Caucasus, were at that period closely linked to Byzantium. Further foundations and the enlargement of small monasteries followed, and the end of the fourteenth century saw the erection of vast monasteries of which Dionysíou, founded by Dionýsios, brother of Theodósios, Archbishop of Trebizond, is an example.

Dionýsios went to Trebizond and there obtained from the Emperor, of the house of Komninós, a document that is still treasured at Dionisíou. This "chrysobull", written in the script common to all such Imperial documents, carries the signature of the Emperor in the purple ink reserved exclusively for the ruler's use. Its special interest and value, however, resides in the full length portraits of the Emperor and Empress that adorn it, clothed as they are in full ceremonial array and carrying the insignia of their office, the crown, the sceptre and the Imperial orb. Between them they hold the foundation charter, rolled, tied with silken bands and sealed with the Gold Seal. Above the Royal figures appears that of St. John the Baptist, patron of the monastery, in an attitude of benediction.

All of these monasteries were founded on the cenobitic principle by which the application of the monastic ideal in every day life concerns the community as a body, under the direction of a superior, the Igoúmenos, elected for life, whose position is roughly equivalent to that of a Western abbot. He is owed obedience and respect by all the monks and presides at the religious services and at the meals that are held in common in the refectory. Under his direction, as spiritual father of them all, the monks live out their lives. Another important difference between the cenobitic system and the idiorhythmic system that came in later is that the property of the monastery and its administration belong to the community as a whole, and no individual member, irrespective of his origin or position, may own property of any description.

This conception of monastic life, transplanted to Athos from the eastern reaches of the Byzantine Empire by St. Athanásios, determined the plan and architecture of the buildings, as we have seen in the chapter on the Great Lávra. It is clearly visible in the photographs of the monasteries of Esphigménou and Kostamonítou. The gently sloping eastern shore of the Peninsula, formed over the centuries by earth brought down by the raging mountain torrents, lends itself admirably to the plan held ideal by the builders of the Great Lávra.

In the interior certain high valleys, too, are suitable, but the configuration of the west coast which, except for its northernmost end, is a succession of wild cliffs plunging straight into the sea, forced radical changes in the masterplan on the builders of the monasteries on the western coast, founded much later than those on the eastern shore.

The Katholikón of Dionysíoú, for example, is crammed into a tunnel-like space between the outer walls and an immense keep that makes the courtyard smaller still. No room at all is left for a detached holy water font. The refectory, as in other houses faced with the same problem, is to be found in one of the wings formed by the outer walls that are built on the monastery's mighty foundations. One of the virtues of these foundations, in themselves walls of enormous size, is somewhat to enlarge the space available at the summit of the crag on which the monastery stands. Nearly two hundred feet above the sea rise tier upon overhanging tier of rooms suspended over the abyss on beams supported by corbels.

Simópetra inevitably brings to mind a heavenly fortress as, high on its cliff above the sea, it climbs straight into the sky. A glimpse of the Katholikón, between the middle and the right hand side of the building, alone betrays the fact that these walls, monstrously deep and strong, and balanced on a crag that looks like a tower, surround a tiny courtyard of which the heart is, as always, the church.

When a guest at Simópetra first steps from his room, situated on the uppermost tier of balconies overlooking the sea, he is liable to leap back in sudden fright. All that stands between him and a plunge into the horrifying void is the floor of a gallery made of thin wooden boards loosely joined together and a flimsy railing surmounted by the frailest of bars. But how wonderful it is to sit here in the evenings, lost in conversation with the monks, while the sun sets in glory behind Olympus and a warm scent-laden evening breeze rises gently from terrassed gardens by the sea.

Advancing centuries marked a steady worsening of the monasteries' financial situation, and a consequent gain of the idiorhythmic idea. By the end of the seventeenth century every monastery had been affected. Later, when times had again improved, the ingrained individualism of the Greek character, added to the unshakable Athonite belief in the superiority of the eremitic form of life, made them cling to the idiorhythmic system in the face of every attempt at reform supported by the Patriarchs of Constantinople.

Problems of various kinds arose out of this situation. The same house sheltered both rich monks and poor monks and even the physical structure of the monasteries was affected. Those that were wealthy and had a greater number of monks expanded until their buildings occupied twice the area, and sometimes more, than had been originally planned. There resulted vast courtyards in which the Katholikón, no longer the centre, was hidden away behind newly erected churches, chapels and administration buildings. Instances of this are Chilandári and Ivíron, once a Georgian, but eventually a purely Greek monastery.

Of the twenty ruling monasteries on Athos eleven follow the cenobitic and nine the idiorhythmic rule.

Cenobitic Monasteries:	Idiorhythmic Monasteries:
Dionysíou	The Great Lávra
Kutloumousíou	Vatopédi
Zográphou	Ivíron
Karakállou	Chilandári
Simópetra	Pandokrátoros
Ayíou Pávlou	Xeropotámou
Grigoríou	Dochiaríou
Esphigménou	Philothéou
Rossikón	Stavronikíta
Kostamonítou	
Xenophóndos	

97 Vissárion, abbot of Grigoríou.

98 420 steps lead from the landing stage to the monastery of Dionysíou.

99 Grigoríou, best kept monastery on Athos.

100 Dionysíou, built on a crag rising straight out of the sea.

101 The Foundation Charter signed by the Emperor Aléxios of Trebizond, dated 1374.

102 Gabriel, abbot and spiritual father of Dionysíou.

103 Esphigménou, situated directly on the sea in a small bay on the east coast of Athos.

104 The sea at the foot of the cliffs in the port of Grigoríou.

105 Simópetra, 1000 feet above the sea, is ten stories high.

106 The Serbian monastery of Chilandári, second most northern on Athos.

107 The priceless Byzantine mosaic Madonna of Chilandári, after its restoration.

108 A monk in his working clothes at the landing stage of Xenophóndos.

109 The Bulgarian monastery of Zográphou, once a famous pilgrimage place and home for incurables.

110 A well preserved icon of St. Peter and St. Paul, at Ivíron.

111 Ivíron, third oldest monastery on Athos, south of Vatopédi on the east coast.

112 Kostamonítou, hidden half way up a valley in the north of the peninsula.

Skite and Hermitages

Dusk was falling as we reached the village of Kafsokalývia after a four hours' march over impracticable mountain paths. We found ourselves in a particularly lovely, well-kept Skití on the southern slopes of the Holy Mountain. The population consisted of some seventy monks, most of them icon painters. At the windows of the small monasteries and behind hedges flowers of all colours bloomed in profusion. Everything was gilded over by the setting sun. The silence was almost tangible, and no one stirred. Following in the wake of our muleteer we presented ourselves to the Archondáris John who was in charge of the guest house. Having attended to the unloading of our mules, Father John ushered us into a dark room that served as a night refuge. Round the walls were benches covered with Turkish rugs. Here, as everywhere else on Athos, the walls were hung with faded portraits of the Greek royal family, of the Patriarch of Constantinople, and of celebrated generals.

After dinner we sat around an open fire and learned of life in the Skite. They had come into being in the sixteenth century when the earlier form of monasticism instituted by St. Athanásios ceased to be practised in the ruling monasteries. Monks, singly or in groups, began leaving the monasteries and built themselves humble shelters in the wilderness. These were called Kéllia. In them three or four monks lived together forming a sort of monastic family. In time some Kéllia joined together to form village communities that gradually evolved a set of rules and a way of life peculiar to themselves.

For over four hundred years successive generations of monks had lived in the Skite and had striven to lead a true monastic life. Our conversation that night and all our subsequent meetings left us convinced of the monks' unswerving loyalty to the ideal of their vocation. It has survived unshaken, and the admirable spirit of brotherly love that is the mainspring of their community life, to say nothing of their heartfelt hospitality, are things that no one who has been their guest can ever forget.

On the following morning clouds like ragged banners swept across the sky above Kafsokalývia. In spite of the storm we decided to put into operation our plan of travelling by the weekly boat to the monastery of Dionysíou, on the west coast. We had waited for two hours by the raging sea before our ship appeared and we were able to board her. This first severe storm after the long hot summer made the trip round the southern cape, always risky, seem doubly dangerous, but it was worth it to us. In spite of the low streaming clouds we could make out, on the face of the cliffs, the shelters of hermits and, towards the north, the little settlements of Karoúlia and Katounákia.

One year later our goal was the Skití of St. Anne. We arrived at Arsanás by boat from Dáphni on a grilling hot summer afternoon towards three o'clock. Apart from our usual luggage we were so laden down with photographic apparatus that we could not have moved a foot without mules. Providence came to our rescue in the form of the monk Pandeleímon who volunteered to see that our luggage reached the Skití. We therefore set off on foot and for an hour climbed steadily under the merciless sun. No breath of air stirred. We toiled on.

The Skití of St. Anne rises in tiers to a height of some two thousand five hundred feet above the sea. About half way up lies the Katholikón, dedicated to St. Anne. It must remain a mystery to every Athos pilgrim how the monks managed to build such an imposing edifice on the narrow, precipitous spur of cliff it occupies. Next to the church stands the house of the Skití's Superior, Father Anthónios, who looks after the Skití's guests and puts them up under his own roof. He is a silent, kindly person much beloved by the village. In true fatherly fashion he set about preparing the evening meal for himself and for his guests. A little later monks began dropping in to discuss with Father Anthoníos problems related to their work. More often than not the question was one of paints and canvas as most of the monks of the Skití are painters. Others are wood carvers, artisans of various kinds, or gardeners. All these interviews took place in an atmosphere that one can only term brotherly, the monks' every action breathing quiet, kindliness, peace. Fascinated, we watched as they pondered and decided upon the plans of their daily life. As each new visitor appeared he greeted us as well as Father Anthónios, and as soon as he heard the word "German" his greeting seemed to take on a special warmth. Curious as to the reason for our popularity in this particular respect, we learned that the Germans are given credit for having saved the monasteries from plunder and violence at the hands of armed marauders in or out of uniform during the Second World War, a German police force having been stationed on Athos for that purpose. When the monks realized that we could speak to them in their own language they were overjoyed and it was late at night before they took their leave. As each monk left he approached the icons and prayed before them, crossing himself repeatedly and reverently kissing the sacred images.

The morning sun comes late to the west coast. Long after the whole of the eastern shore is bathed in sunlight, the high bristling range of Athos holds back the day from the Skití of St. Anne. From the balcony of our room we watched the dark surface of the water become touched here and there with flecks of the most delicate light. Minute by minute the sun's brilliant arms reached further over the sea, awakening all the dormant richness of its colours. The towering western flank of Athos, was one great featureless wall of blackness, unrelieved, forbidding and sombre beyond belief. Gradually, under the magic fingers of light, it became transformed before our eyes, taking on a thousand shapes and all the colours of creation. Monastic houses emerged from the shadows and soon we could make out the figures of monks already engaged on their daily tasks. Peacefully they moved about their narrow, terraced gardens, planting, digging, weeding, letting water stored in great containers flow into the network of ditches that irrigate their vegetable gardens. Others repaired walls and fences, others were busy with their beasts of burden. They seemed to be wearing, in the day's work, the cloak of prayer and silence they had woven at prayer, in church.

To the south of the Skití of St. Anne, at the foot of the Holy Mountain, there still live hermits. Their cells are so cleverly hidden away in the clefts of mountains and in the heart of forests that it is virtually impossible for a tourist to find one out. The boyhood friend of one of these hermits entrusted us with a letter which we were to deliver personally. A monk of the Skití sent ahead word of our intended visit and then led us over boulders and mountain torrents, through dense undergrowth and along the brink of chasms to the spot where stood the bare, clean little hut. A patriarchal old man with snow white hair greeted us in smiling silence. For the past twenty five years he had used the gift of speech only to pray or to sing religious chant. The whole of his ascetic figure, but especially his eyes, radiated goodness. We were introduced by our guide in a few whispered words. The hermit remained silent. The cell was alive with the pungent smell of herbs. Water boiled in a rusty kettle suspended over the open fire. The old man offered us the traditional welcome of tea, spring water, figs and bread. As we handed him the letter from his friend he bowed deeply and crossed himself, and when we took our leave, those extraordinary eyes, alert and full of a joyful gratitude, rested on us radiant and strong with blessings.

Our encounter with the silent, emaciated old man, wholly given over to the spirit, is one we shall not soon forget. Had we perhaps been in the presence of a saint? One of the chosen of God? For years he had roamed the world in search of a place where his vocation might be fulfilled, had found it and had lived over forty years in absolute solitude and poverty. He, like the other hermits of the Holy Mountain, had deliberately chosen a life of the utmost rigour and asceticism, and of prayer at the foot of the Cross that their — and our — sins be forgiven and that we be admitted to the Kingdom of Heaven.

117 Hermit or "fool in Christ"?

118 Monastic cells, some fallen into disrepair, in the Skití of St. Anne.

119 The Skití of St. Anne rises to a height of some 2500 feet above the sea.

120 One of the perfectly tended vegetable gardens on which the monks depend for a living.

121 A monk drawing cool spring water by means of a water wheel.

122 The impressive face of a monk of the Skití.

123 The picturesque slate roofs of kitchen and refectory.

124 Monks at the great Easter Dinner, wearing their ceremonial veils.

126 A novice washing up in the guest house kitchen.

127 View from a monastery window of scattered cells of the Skití.

128 Father Seraphim, monk and priest of the Skití of St. Anne, with his "family" in the house chapel.

129 A richly carved iconostasis and icons of various kinds in one of the smaller monasteries.

130 A hermit monk in the choir of a chapel where once several monks had joined in prayer.

131 Father Dionýsios, priest and monk, leads the chant and is an icon painter of the Skití of St. Anne.

132 The "Great Schima", an embroidered scapular bestowed on rigourously ascetic monks by a Spiritual Father. (For translation see page 225.)

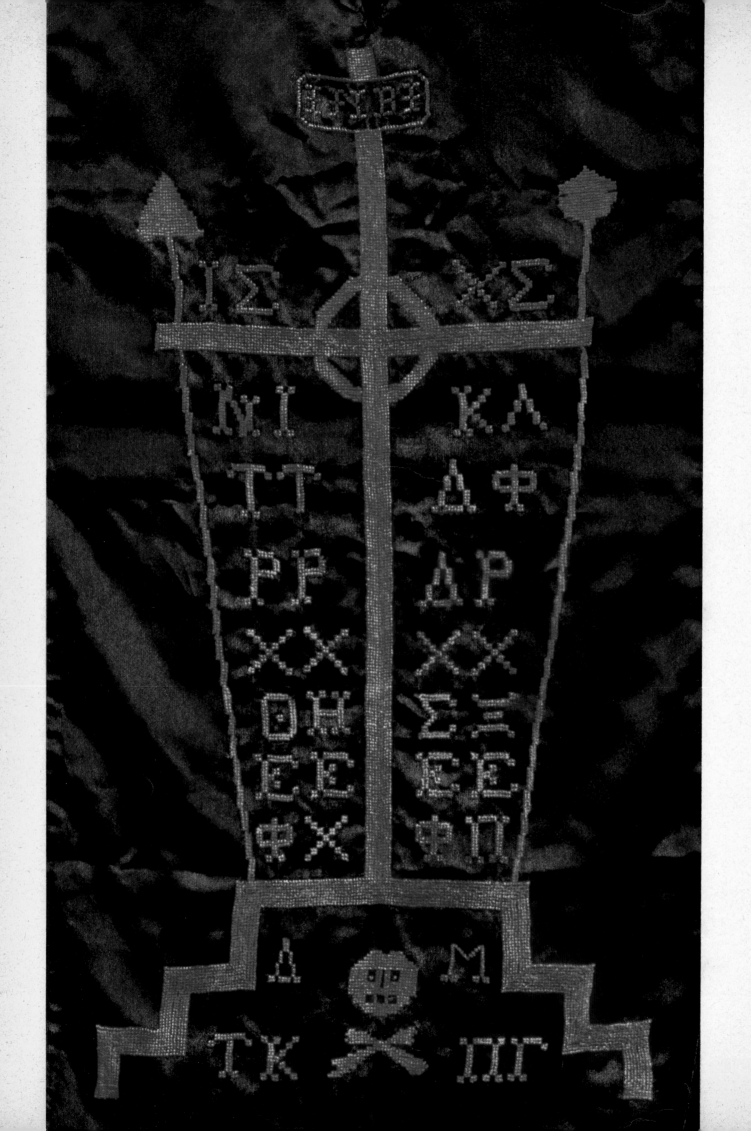

Icons and their Painters

One morning, at the Skití of St. Anne, we rose at five o'clock only to find Father Seraphim, the Superior of the small monastery where we were staying, already at his easel. The first light of morning streamed through the great windows bathing him in light. What a charming picture he made, the venerable Father Seraphim who had completely won our hearts. He was a man of genuine humility, and a gifted artist with a vigorous spiritual life. As we stood hesitantly by the door, fearing to disturb him at his work, he turned his head, greeted us with a cheerful "Good Morning" and invited us in. Icons painted by Father Seraphim in the last few months lay about on benches and stools. On the walls hung ancient icons such as we had seen adorning iconostases and sanctuaries all over Athos.

We had often seen icons, strong ancient paintings representing Saints of the Eastern Church, in museums, at exhibitions, and especially, while serving with the German army medical corps, in the houses and churches of Russia, where the face of Christ the Ruler of all Things, of the Mother of God, of an angel or of a saint loomed towards us out of a mystical darkness. Good books on icons, recently published and, we should like to believe, our own modest efforts, had done much in the last few decades to reveal the deep symbolic content of this ancient form of painting. But what Father Seraphim showed us that morning had little if any connection with the genuine tradition of icon painting. Why, we could not help asking ourselves, does he call his pictures of saints, painted with a smooth sweetness that leaves men of our time absolutely cold and positively repels connoisseurs, "icons"? The authentic tradition, scrupulously handed on through so many centuries, seems not to have reached the teachers of Father Seraphim and of the present generation of painters on Athos. At some period monks began to produce pious, colourful pictures according to their own taste and inspiration and called them "icons" although, by the way they were painted, they did not fulfil the essential demands of the holy art. Thus most of the artists painting on Athos today are quite unaware of a great opportunity and simply pass it by: that of giving to the world icons steeped in the vigorous spiritual life of the Eastern Church.

Nikolai Leskow, in his short story "The Sealed Angel", makes us experience the Russian faith in the efficacy of an icon. A group of carpenters travels through Russia carrying the icon of an angel with them. The angel himself is present in the painting and his celestial power guards the carpenters from all evil. When the icon disappears from among them they are deserted by their angel. Now without his protection their community is handed over to the evil spirit. Ill fortune threatens their work. Only after the icon has returned to them are they able to live at peace and work together, since the angel is in their midst. Made happy they once again experience the protection of his mighty wings.

The faithful of the Eastern Church approach their icons with a touching fervour and intimacy that seem strange to us Christians of the West. On entering a church the Athonite monks bow low before the icons, kiss them and make the sign of the Cross again and again, for they are not kissing a picture but the Mother of God or Christ himself. The first centuries of Christianity evolved certain types of pictures whose origins are veiled in a darkness at least partly mystical. Ancient legends relate, for instance, that they were not the product of human hands. The Church was believed to have received its first portrait of Christ from the Lord Himself and the inscription on the modern copies still reads: "The painting of the Lord not done by man's hand." Similarly the Mother of God is said to have brought about a painting of herself in a miraculous manner.

The painting of icons from the earliest times had to be carried out under certain conditions and made specific demands on the painters. Ancient Byzantine and Russian icons were not painted by monks according to their own fancy but by order of the Church and to the accompaniment of fasts and prayers. The artist, who was also a monk, stood humbly before the Fathers and was empowered by them, as his spiritual masters, to paint an icon. A special blessing was imparted to him on the occasion. The more he was filled with the "Pneuma" or Spirit of the living God, the greater would be his power to make tangible to men, in a form fixed once for all long ago in the past, the saint or the angel he had been chosen to portray.

Rules governing the actual technique of painting had been drawn up and fixed very early, and were then handed down reverently through the centuries. The "Erminía", the ancient book of instructions for Athos painters, describes them at length. Some of these are stressed as having particular importance: first of all, a chalk-like foundation must be laid on a well seasoned wooden panel. On this the painter draws his picture in very fine lines. The face and hands and certain parts of the dress or special symbols pertaining to the saint such as a roll, a book, or a cross, receive a further coating or foundation. The colours themselves are made from stones and other natural products ground to a very fine powder. They are mixed with yolk of egg and bound with size, and then applied to the foundation which in the meantime had been allowed to dry. The background is covered with gold leaf and the more important outlines of each figure emphasized by the means of fine gold lines. As a result of all this the icons attained a mysterious, transcendental splendour that conveyed to the faithful the light of another world.

We were surprised to meet, in a small monastery on the east coast, a young monk who had mastered all the precepts of the ancients, and whose icons, truly worthy of the name, grew as if with a strength inspired by the Holy Spirit, out of the deep bosom of the Church. We learned that the Superior of his monastery had taken him some years previously to a master painter of icons at Athens. There, during a long and painstaking apprenticeship, he was introduced into the mysteries of the art of iconography. The icons of this gifted young painter, which we saw on our visits to his studio, display an extraordinary grasp of the ancient forms and prototypes, a great intimacy of expression and a splendid vigour in the colouring. We are tempted to believe that we have discovered in him a painter who, together with his pupils, is capable of bringing the genuine art of icon painting on Athos to a new blossoming.

The churches and monasteries of Athos are so characterised by the visual presence of the saints that, stripped of icons, they would be shorn of their essential meaning as well. The church, covered from floor to ceiling and far up in the cupola with pictures of saints, is united through them to the realm of heaven, a realm to which the monks know they are admitted whenever they join in their choir office to praise the Almighty, present among them in the Blessed Sacrament and in the icons that surround them.

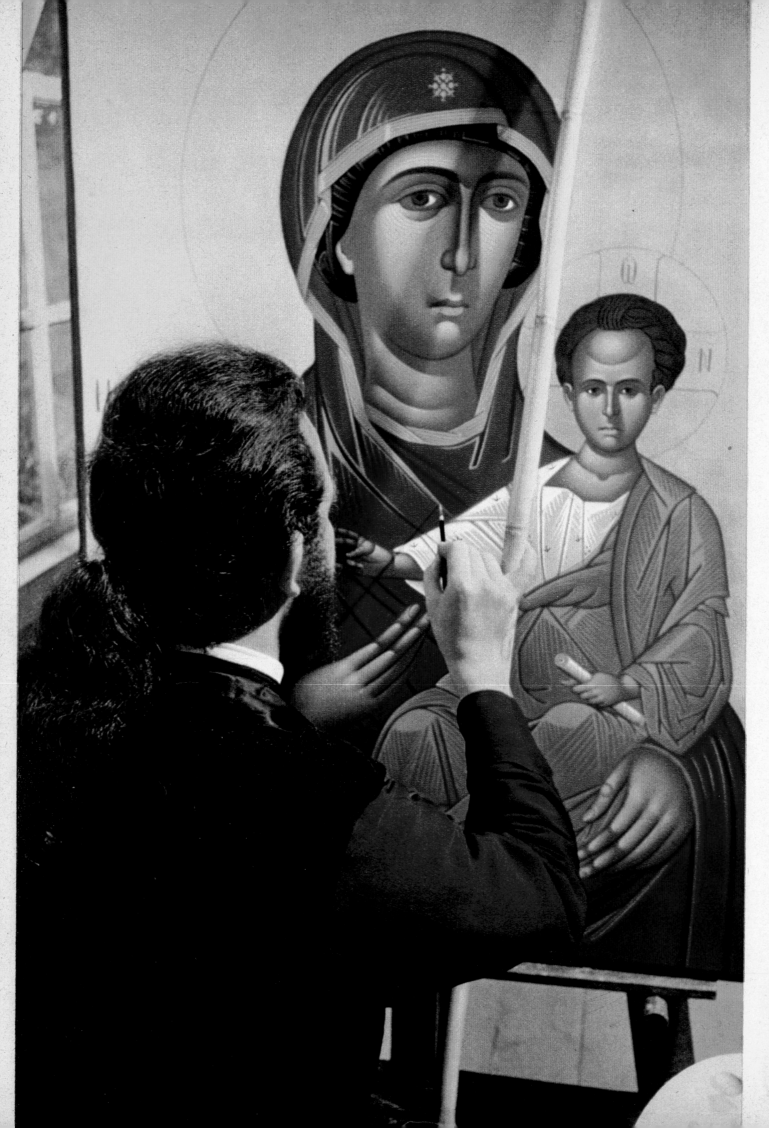

144

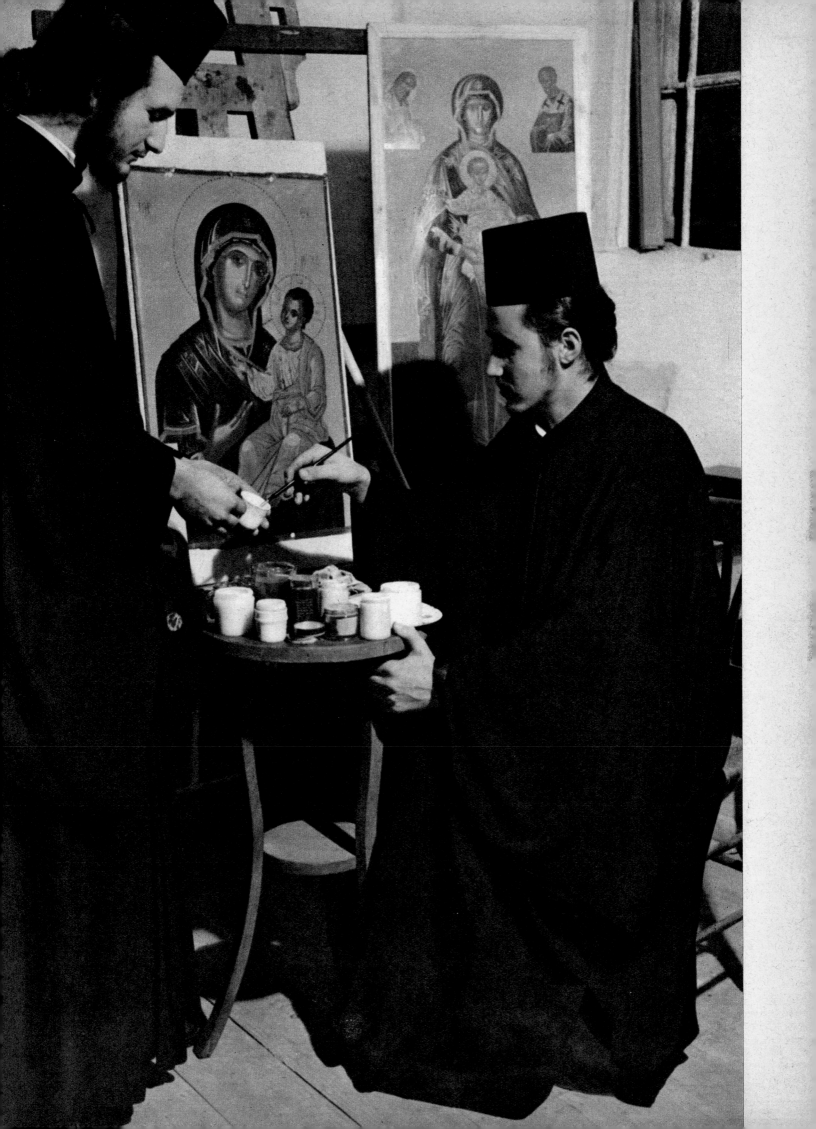

The Katholikón

The Katholikón, or main church of a monastery, is used for the religious services in which the community as a whole take part. Often, despite its considerable size, its interior is divided by so many walls pierced only by doors that at a first glance it appears to be more a succession of comparatively small rooms rather than a large church. The divisions are not arbitrary, however, and it soon becomes evident that by their means the building is well adapted to the rather complicated Byzantine cult.

Before setting foot in the church proper two rooms, the Exo- and the Esonarthex, that is the outer and the inner narthex, must be traversed. Sometimes they are preceded by a hall that is either open, like a loggia, or closed with large glass windows. These first rooms are not intended as antichambers where the faithful may prepare for the atmosphere of the House of God, but have a function of their own. They are furnished with choir stalls set against the frescoed walls, and regularly certain parts of the choir office are said there. They are also the scene of special consecrations on the occasion of major religious celebrations throughout the year.

Some monks prefer to penetrate no further into the church than the narthex and, remaining in one of the high, narrow choir stalls to devote themselves undisturbed to their personal prayers. This is often the case of uneducated monks who, understanding little or nothing of the Church language, fill in the long hours of the choir service with a kind of rosary.

The interior of the church proper is equally strange to a Western visitor. Numbers of large candelabra bristling with candles, stands bearing icons, and lecterns of various heights are strewn over the floor that is inlaid with coloured marble. The walls are covered from top to bottom with sequences and cycles of paintings that are continued in the numerous cupolas. The central cupola, which is also the highest and largest, usually displays an immense image of the Pantocrator, the glorified Christ represented as Ruler of all Things. The Incarnate Word of God holds in His left hand the Book of Life while His right is lifted in the Byzantine gesture of benediction. His face is one of majestic severity but, as the Patriarch Phótios has pointed out, it is of a severity that can terrify only the guilty, but not a man who is free from sin. The monk knows full well that he stands in the shadow of the Judgement of God but his trust is in the mercy of the Saviour whom he has vowed to follow and imitate his whole life long. Apart from frescoes, every wall pillar and column, and in many cases the space above the choir stalls that extend all round the church, are hung with icons, the characteristic paintings of the Eastern Church which were the subject of our last chapter.

The strangest sight for the non-Byzantine in every Katholikón is, however, the Témblon or iconostasis, a wall of pictures. Originally, the iconostasis was a marble choir screen such as is still to be seen in the Protáton, the main church of Karyés, where it is veiled only by light curtains. In other churches time and the constant addition of icons hung in rows one above the other have turned it into a wall pierced only by three doors. The door on the left leads to the Proskomidí, a room furnished with a small altar table on which are laid out the sacred vessels and offerings for the celebration of Mass. The door on the right leads to a similar room where liturgical vestments, vessels and instruments are stored. The central, larger, so-called "Royal Door", normally closed by a pair of half-doors ornamented with a painting of the Annunciation, gives access to the Sanctuary proper.

Inside the Sanctuary, under a canopy frequently richly carved and gilded, stands the "Holy Table" which in turn carries a simple rectangular tabernacle containing the Most Blessed Sacrament. The altar is further adorned with candlesticks, the book of the Gospels, and, more often than not, one or more particularly precious icons. Behind the altar there usually stands a cross in the Byzantine manner, that is, a flat crucifix painted, never carved, on a wooden board that is cut following the shape of the Body. Further back still, against the wall of the apse there is often an ancient bishop's throne, in fact no longer used today and "occupied" by an icon that is held in special veneration.

From the outside, the first two sections of the church are recognisable by their pairs of smaller cupolas and the main inner room by its central, larger cupola. The three divisions of the Sanctuary can be identified by a medium sized, rounded apse and two flanking, less prominent apses, at the east end of the church. Finally two apses in the north and the south of the main inner room denote the situation of the two choirs.

Opposite:

Elevation and ground plan of the Katholikón of Chilandári. These illustrate the special position of the Exo- and Esonarthex as well as the position of the cupolas, and of the Sanctuary with its altar table, behind the iconostasis.

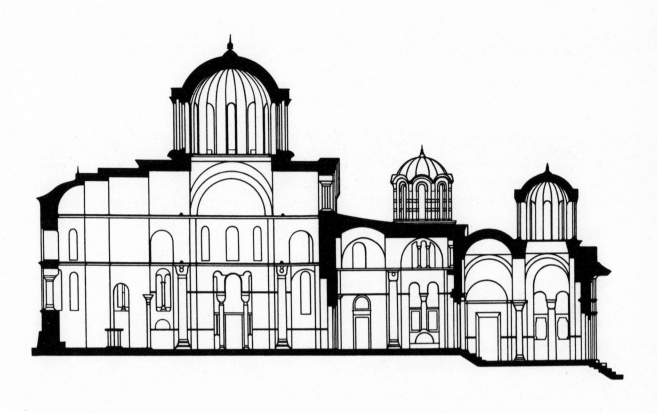

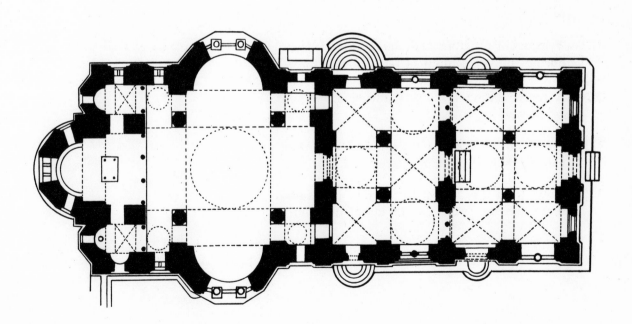

155

Easter

The night was cold but no one seemed to notice it. All attention, all thought centered on the little group in shimmering vestments that stood out against a sombre background formed by a semi-circle of dark clad monks. In the soft light of the honey scented wax candles each of us carried, only faces were visible, small flecks of light between the darkness of beard and the black veil that hung from the monks' tall hats over forehead and shoulders. An expression as of tension relaxed shone on all these faces, of the fulfilment of a hope that, gathering strength through forty days of the most severe fasts had reached its highest, almost unbearable pitch during the celebration of the Easter liturgy. At Mass, the precentors had sung after each verse of the Eighty First psalm: "God stands in the congregation of the princes. He judgeth among the gods." And we had answered: "Arise, O Lord, and judge the world, for Thou shalt inherit all nations." Ever stronger, ever more urgent the call had sounded and now the moment of fulfilment had come.

On the stroke of midnight the Bishop had appeared in the Royal Door of the iconostasis wearing brilliantly embroidered vestments and the episcopal stole of shimmering white silk. On his head was the golden crown-like mitre and in his hand he carried the lighted Easter candle. As the precentors entoned: "Come, take light of the light that knows no darkness and praise Christ Who rose from the dead", we had advanced one by one to light our candle at that of the Bishop.

The deacons, splendid in their festive vestments, surrounded the Bishop holding their candles on high. To the singing of: "The angels in heaven proclaim Thy Resurrection, Christ and Saviour. We on earth beseech Thee cleanse our hearts that we too may be worthy to sing Thy praises", a procession had formed and moved slowly out of the church. Under the open sky the Bishop announced the Resurrection to the assembled people in the words of the angel to the women at the grave: "You seek Jesus of Nazareth who was crucified: He is risen." As the Bishop's voice rose, entoning the song of victory, the joy of Easter was reflected on all the faces in the crowd. They joined their exultant voices to his and sang over and over again: "Christós anésti ek nekrôn. Christ hath risen from the dead, by death trampling upon death, and upon those in the tombs He hath bestowed life."

After a number of hymns and prayers we re-entered the church to find that all the candles of the vast wheel-like candelabra and of the stands had been lit, as well as all the oil lamps that burn before the icons. There seemed to be thousands of sources of light yet even when the candles we all bore added their radiance to that which already filled the church, the light was not the unwavering, cold visibility that invades our Western churches at the celebration of high feasts. For all the myriad small flames, the church remained clothed in a mystical half light that seemed to flow like a translucent veil from the cupola above us down the frescoed walls. The brocade of the deacon's vestments as he stood before the iconostasis during the litanies and the silken splendour of the Bishop's robes shone with a much more subtle richness in the light of the candelabra than they would have done in the soulless glare of electric light.

A soft glow that seemed to radiate from within rather than to have been borrowed from any outside source, was imparted to the faces of the monks in their choir stalls as the precentors entoned the sublime Easter hymn: "The day of Resurrection! Rejoice, all the peoples of the earth! Pascha, Easter of the Lord! For Christ our Lord Whose praises we sing has brought us out of death to life, from earth to heaven." The devotion of His people clothed the Redeemer in an aura as golden as the great nimbus that surrounded the image of the Pantocrator, victorious over life and death, the Judge of the World who looked down on us from the apex of the cupola.

The night's ceremonies close with solemn High Mass. On Easter Sunday there are no religious services as a rest after the extremely strenuous days of Holy Week, until, towards evening, the monks gather in church to sing Vespers. On this occasion, the Gospel of the Resurrection is read aloud in as many languages as possible: in Greek by the Bishop, by the priests and deacons in Latin, Russian, Roumanian, and even, in memory of the days when Athos lived under the yoke of Turkish domination, in Turkish. On this occasion a scene imbued with the true spirit of Easter is enacted. Each monk approaches the Bishop and exchanges with him the Easter greeting. He then exchanges the same greeting with each of his brethren in turn. On this day the kiss of brotherhood may be refused to no one, no matter for what reason. At Easter every antipathy, every enmity must be buried to the singing of the hymn: "Day of Resurrection! Let us embrace on this feast and say to each other 'brother' even to those who hate us. Let us forgive in the name of the Resurrection!" Hence the name "Esperinós tis agápis" Vespers of brotherly love.

Following Vespers the whole community, headed by the Bishop, the priests and deacons, all still clad in their glittering robes, moves in procession to the Council room of the Government Building where a final ceremony takes place and sweets, coffee, liqueurs, and Easter eggs dyed crimson are served to everyone.

The whole of Easter Monday is loud with the pealing of bells that ring ceaselessly from the low, heavy tower by the Protáton. This joyful shattering of silence is in honour of the miraculous image of Our Lady that is carried in procession every year on this day. According to legend it was before this image of Our Lady that the Archangel Gabriel taught a pious devotee the "Axión estin", most noble of hymns to the Virgin Mary: "Axión estin — it is truly right and just to praise Thee, Mother of God, ever blessed and immaculate."

As the Mother of the Saviour, Mary had participated in most sorrowful fashion in the suffering of the Passion that redeemed mankind. On Good Friday it had been said of her: "Today, O Saviour of the world, the Virgin immaculate saw Thee hanging from the Cross. She, Thy Mother, was overwhelmed with sorrow and her heart was wounded with most bitter wounds." But during the night of Easter, the precentors call out to her: "Rejoice most pure Virgin, rejoice, full of grace, rejoice most blessed among women! Thy Son is risen on the third day!"

On Monday her image is carried in triumph through a land bursting into bloom under the Easter sun. The bells, rung in the Greek fashion by striking the fixed bells with small iron hammers or their fixed tongues, send forth a volley of sound more joyous than solemn. An old Russian monk, beating the Símandron in time to the song, strides at the head of the milling, colourful throng, composed of priests and deacons in splendid vestments, monks in their wide flowing robes, policemen and their officers in uniform and laymen in their somewhat threadbare Sunday best. The population lines up before the houses, priests carry icons and deacons carry censers, while ordinary monks carry dark, squat bottles with long thin necks out of which they shake oil of roses, sprinkling it over the procession as it passes by. Late in the afternoon the procession regains the church where solemn Vespers bring the feast of Easter to a final close.

Mountain of Light

The sun had been beating down mercilessly on the Holy Mountain for over a week when, one afternoon towards five o'clock, we left the Great Lávra with the intention of climbing to its summit. An uncomfortable ride of some three hours brought us to Kerasiá "the place of the cherry trees", last of the small monastic settlements before the final climb. The date was the twenty-third of June and the monks were engaged in picking cherries. Instead of the usual drink of welcome they brought us a heaping bowl of the ripe delicious fruit. We rested for an hour and set off again, a new moon riding lightly in the sky. One of the monks had kindly offered to guide us to a point from where we could hardly fail to find our way. Through clinging underbrush, over patches of scree and boulders and on the edge of precipices, we picked our way along the path that was often barely visible. After two hours of scrambling we were brought up short before a high, dark building. This could only be the shrine of the Panayía, of Our Lady, described to us by the monks at Kerasiá as lying about one thousand two hundred feet below the summit, and the place where we had decided to rest before the final ascent. Beyond the portal that gave access to the abandoned monastery we found the cistern, the praises of whose cool waters we had heard sung by countless monks. By the light of our electric flash-lights we drew a pail of water from a deep cleft in the rock. Long, slow, deliciously cold draughts of it seemed to wash every trace of weariness from our bodies and we decided there and then to reverse our former decision and to push on immediately and spend the rest of the night on the summit. Cautiously we climbed through the trackless, rocky wilderness, over cliffs that seemed perpendicular in the darkness, zig-zagging where we could up the rough, relentlessly steep incline. We lost all track of time but after what could not have been more than one hour we found ourselves confronted with a building that materialised suddenly out of the dark. Cautiously we felt our way round the solid yet strangely ghost-like walls, to find that we were actually standing on the summit of the Holy Mountain. The building was the Chapel of the Transfiguration, that most ancient and beloved shrine of Athos. All around us the earth swept steeply, swiftly down to the sea, lost in silence over six thousand feet below. Above our heads was nothing but the silent night. It took us some time to realize that we really stood on the peak that had acted on us like a magnet ever since we had first seen it. Who could count the number of times our eyes had lifted, irresistibly, to rest on its outline chiselled against a brilliant mediterranean sky or on the soft grey clouds that veiled it? On foot, on muleback, from on board ship, out of a monastery window, our eyes had searched for and always found, the Holy Mountain. And now at last we stood upon it.

Down in Kerasiá, and during the ascent, we had hardly been able to breathe for the heat, but here, on the peak, the rarefied air was glacial. Forcing the door to the chapel we found ourselves in a musty, dilapidated room. We examined our surroundings by the light of a wax candle and found the remains of ancient choir stalls and a small iconostasis, and also evidence of the repairs carried out in recent years by hermits in an endeavour to save the chapel from complete disintegration.

We took shelter within its walls for a while until, towards three o'clock, the cold drove us forth. A change had come over everything. At midnight the slender sickle of the moon had sailed above our heads. Now it was balanced on the silver, shimmering horizon. We sat on a boulder before the chapel and gazed eastwards, waiting for the rising of the sun into a sky that already, almost imperceptibly, was preparing to shed the cloak of night. Below us slept the land of monks.

But not the monks themselves. Already they would have taken their places in the choir stalls of churches and chapels, in the monasteries, Kéllia and in the Skite. Engrossed in their long services, they would be praying. Only tourists, or workmen, slept. It was always in the night hours that demons and spirits that fear the light have been busy in the world of men. Against them, like a phalanx formed up and ready to give battle, stood the monks, lifting their hands to God as Moses had done on Mount Sinai. As often as Moses had let fall his arms the Israelites had fallen back before their enemies. Were the monks to cease lifting their hands to God as they lifted them this night and every night, the demons would fall on them and put out the fire of their inner strength. Therefore did they pray, ceaselessly, for the peace of the world. The higher and more glowing their love of God and man the greater the strength with which they could draw down on to earth the peace of Heaven.

At about this same hour the monks of the West would also be filing into their churches for Vigils — the night watch — and the rhythmic interchange of psalms and hymns. "O Lord, open thou my lips, and my mouth shall show forth thy praise." On the summit of the Holy Mountain we opened our breviaries and joined them in their prayers: "Why O Lord are they multiplied that afflict me? Many are they who rise up against me. Many say to my soul: there is no salvation for him in his God. But Thou, O Lord are my protector, my glory, and the lifter up of my head. I have cried to the Lord with my voice and He hath heard me from His holy hill. I have slept and have taken my rest: and I have risen up because the Lord hath protected me. I will not fear thousands of the people surrounding me. Arise, O Lord; save me O my God. For Thou hast struck all them who are my adversaries without cause: Thou hast broken the teeth of sinners. Salvation is of the Lord: and Thy blessing is upon Thy people."

The land below us lay like a sleeping monster, but as our prayers were mingled with those of our brethren from the East and from the West we saw how the growing light changed its threatening form, slowly turning it into a land awake and at peace. The east was rent with slender spears of light that pierced infinity, announcing the coming of the sun. Fascinated, we stared across those fabled seas to where a thin, blood-red line appeared. Majestically the sun rose from beyond the rim of the world and, as if in answer to the prayers that had filled the night, the whole peninsula was bathed in a silver radiance. The light of Tabor seemed to shine again, letting fall its rays on the land of monks from the height of the Holy Mountain.

It was the feast of St. John the Baptist, and the sun shone on monasteries, gardens, and cemeteries, on the living and on the dead whose bones, three years after burial, are brought out of the darkness of the grave and placed in ossuaries for all to see. Skulls and bones hold no terrors on Athos. They are merely another phase of life, like prayer and meditation, like work and sleep. It has always been true that the stronger the belief in the Resurrection, the less did Christians fear death or the sight of human skeletons. As to the monks of Athos, they live in the unshakable belief that it is only through the privations of their ascetic lives and the unending toil of their ceaseless prayers that they will achieve a spiritual strength capable of defeating the demons and, by overcoming the downward drag of the human body, transfuse it with everlasting light. Carrying their daily cross they ascend, step by step, towards the light that shines on Tabor until they cross the threshold of eternity. There await them the "Mystical Banquet", the company of all the saints, and their Lord Jesus Christ.

197 Painting in the monastery of Ivíron. The Transfiguration of Christ. Mount Athos is represented as being Mount Tabor.

198 View from the summit of Mount Athos at sunrise, towards 4.30 a. m.

200 Father Efthýmíos shortly before his death.

201 Painting in the monastery of Esphigménou representing the monastic life: the monk stretched on his cross is tempted and tortured by demons.

202 A monk ascends the steps of his monastery, a symbol of his other, spiritual ascent towards the life of transfiguration.

203 Ancient painting on parchment at the monastery of Dionysíou: the soul of the dying monk issues from his mouth and is carried away by the Archangel Michael, the Angel of Death.

204 The cemetery of the monastery of Dionysiou and Father Efthýmios grave.

206 The sun on the monastery roofs. Under the arches the bones of the dead await the shining of eternal light.

207 Death holds no terrors for this smiling monk.

208 Large fresco on the refectory wall at Dionysíou. Left: the Judge of the World above a choir of angels and the fallen Lucifer. Right: the ladder of Heaven with ascending and descending monks and devils.

210 Fifteenth century fresco in the refectory of the Great Lávra: "The Mystical Banquet". Christ and the Disciples at the Last Supper.

212 Sunrise at the summit of Mount Athos. The light of transfiguration falls on the Holy Mountain.

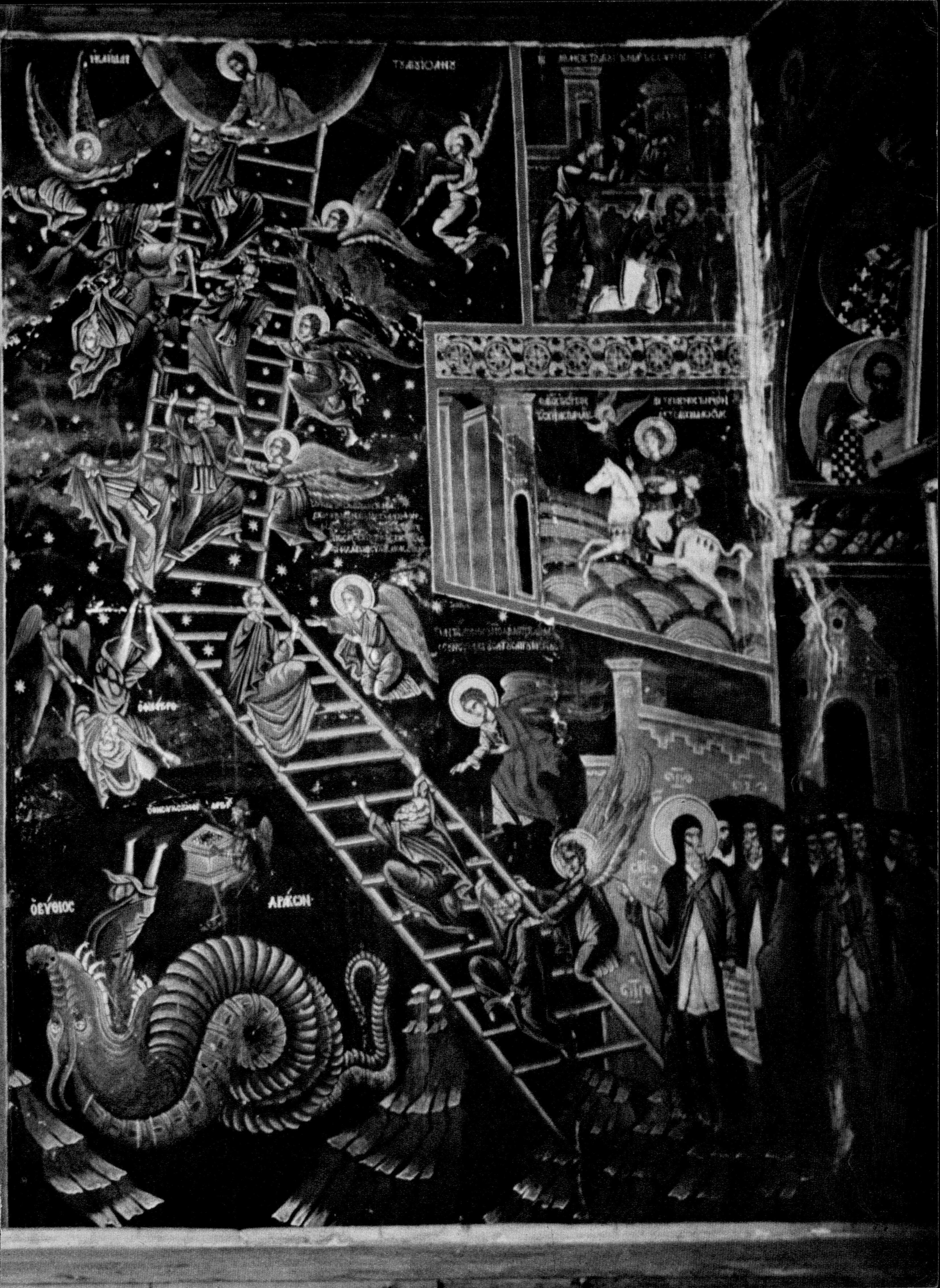
ΔΡΑΚΩΝ

Ὁ ΜΥCΤΙΚΟ
ΙC.

ΔΕΙΠΝΟC.

χ̅c̅.

On the Eastern Monastic Technique of Meditation and Breath Control (The Jesus Prayer)

The ideal of the first monks, who lived as hermits in the desert, was to pray without ceasing. Even during their long hours of bodily toil they observed the custom of repeating continuously some short form of prayer. The name "Jesus" often recurred in their prayers and later it became the custom to add the name of Jesus to more and more invocations.

The "Jesus Prayer" as it was finally called, did not attain a fixed formula for a very long time, and the bodily exercises that were later connected with it are first mentioned in a short work by Nikiphóros, a monk of Athos in the fourteenth century. In his book the author recommends a technique, affecting both body and soul that, he maintains, is a valuable aid to concentration. "If thou wouldst pray" he writes, "shut fast the door of thy cell, become quite calm, seat thyself, and with head bowed on thy breast contemplate thy navel, let thy spirit seek where thy heart dwells that it may be present in thy mind as thou repeatest the invocation of Jesus Christ." Nikiphóros is the author of another treatise "On Guarding the Heart", that commends the reader, by breathing to transpose his spirit into his heart and there to cry continually: "Lord Jesus Christ, Son of God, have mercy upon me!" Here for the first time we find the Jesus Prayer in the form it has since preserved.

Together with the Jesus Prayer this technique found its way to Athos where it has been practised to an ever increasing extent. Gregory of Sinai (+ 1346) who lived for some time on Athos, advises his pupils: "Seat thyself upon a low seat, draw down thy consciousness from thy head to thy heart and hold it firmly there. Then, painfully bowed down, cry with heart and spirit: Lord Jesus Christ have mercy upon me!" Athos soon became a centre of the Jesus Prayer and of the bodily exercises connected with it. Above all it was expounded and defended by the celebrated Gregory Palamás (1296—1359) and, in 1351, the interpretation he supported — known as Hesychasm — was declared the official doctrine of the Byzantine Church. From then on Athos remained undisturbed in the practice of the Jesus Prayer, which spread from there through the whole Byzantine Church as far as Russia. This "mystical and spiritual prayer" as it was called, became a striking characteristic of Byzantine monks, an original creation in which the attitude of the body, the control of breathing and the repetition of a name draw together all the powers of body and soul and so lead the whole man to God.

This prayer of the heart continues to be practised with great fervour on Athos, whether in the silence of the cell or during the many occupations of the monastic life. In his cell the monk usually begins by praying with his lips and then only with his spirit. He adapts his prayer to the rhythm of his breathing, saying as he breathes in: "Lord Jesus Christ, Son of God", and, as he breathes out: "Have mercy upon me!" The masters of the spiritual life insist that during the practice of the Jesus Prayer one must remain attached to Christ in faith and love. If this condition is fulfilled the prayer will become a habit that naturally accompanies breathing during the day and at night and during the various occupations of daily life, or even while one is engaged in conversation.

It must be stressed that the Jesus Prayer does not set itself up as a substitute for serious Christian asceticism. On the contrary, from the very beginning it was closely allied to "concentration, vigilance and sobriety". The Hesychasts knew very well that union with God is a free gift of love from the Almighty, and that it cannot be obtained by any technique however elaborate. But, like the ancients of India, they knew that body and soul are inextricably bound together, each activity of the soul having its repercussions on the body, while the attitudes of the body have in turn an effect on the life of the soul. Finally, they were aware that the concepts "Name", "Breath", and "Heart" are mysteries that play a vital role in our lives, something the moderns are beginning to rediscover.

The monks of Athos recommend the practice of the "spiritual and mystical prayer" to the laity but they insist that it is essential while practising it to abstain from all excess in eating and drinking, to lead a serious Christian life and to hold oneself apart from the temptations of the world.

Dom Athanasius van Ruijven, Chevetogne.

The Monastic Chant of the Eastern Church
(Note to Accompany the Record)

Since the first beginnings of Christianity, singing has had an important place in daily worship. It is not easy to determine what was originally the precise nature of this chant. But if we remember that Jesus and his disciples sang a hymn after the Last Supper (Matth. 26:30), and if we recall that St. Paul was accustomed to proclaim the Gospel in synagogues, we may assume that the chant of the first Christian communities was essentially that of the Synagogue and more especially of the Hellenistic Synagogue, that is, a kind of chant in which Hebrew and Hellenistic elements were probably blended. As far as I know, no document containing Christian music of this early period has survived. Indeed, even the oldest Byzantine musical notation, transmitted by manuscripts which do not go back beyond the early Middle Ages, has so far resisted all efforts to decipher it.

Roughly at this time (in the ninth century) missions to the Slavs began and it seems now to be established that the Slavs took over from their missionaries not only their creed but also their Greek — that is Byzantine — chant. But here also we come up against the difficulty that the ancient Slavonic manuscripts with musical notation are no longer legible. A few scholars are active in this field and one may hope that they will arrive at positive results in a not too distant future. It is even possible that the Slavonic documents may give us the key to the riddle of ancient Byzantine musical notation.

Like every living thing, the chant of the Eastern Church, Slavonic as well as Greek, has developed in the course of time and not everywhere along the same lines. The traditional Greek music has no doubt been influenced by that of the Arabs and Turks, though to how great an extent is a very controversial question. Most Western scholars — not the Greeks, be it noted — ascribe to these influences the extraordinary diversity of modes, scales and "corruptions" (i. e., the amazing possibilities for augmenting and diminishing intervals), and suggest that the vocal effects, so characteristic of this type of chant, but so strange to the Western ear, derive from the same source. However that may be, it is this unison chant, very complex, purely melodic, conveying a deeply religious impression to the experienced ear, that is the only one practised in the Greek monasteries of Athos. The same chant, with little alteration, is in general use among the Bulgarians, who sing in Church Slavonic and among the Roumanians who use their own language.

Among the Orthodox Slavs other than the Bulgarians, Church music has been exposed to the most widely varying influences, those of Western Europe proving particularly active. These influences, coupled with the laws of internal development, have produced at least the following main kinds of chant: Serbian, Pod-Carpathian, and West Ukrainian, that of Kiev and finally the various Great Russian types, for instance the magnificent but somewhat austere "znamennyi rospev". Russian Church music during the last 400 years has been subject to influence from Western Europe, especially to that of Italian polyphonic singing, to such an extent that one can say that almost without exception in the Russian Church today and in the Russian monasteries on Mt. Athos the chant is polyphonic.

Thanks to this Western European imprint on Russian music, the non-Russian can understand and enjoy it without difficulty. Moreover, for some years now, it has become widely known through records, though it must be recognised that these have not always given us the best music from a religious point of view. Prescinding from the question of mixed choirs, even the well known male choirs are of a quite different character from those of the Russian monasteries on Athos. In the first place, these latter are not schools of music but places of prayer and penitence, and secondly, the dedication to God of each individual monk as well as of the whole monastery, lends to the choir office and to the chant a distinctive, intimate quality that is immediately perceptible, but hard to define. Technically and vocally the chant of the monks is certainly inferior to that of the famous choirs, but one will find that its effect through its very simplicity is all the more elevating. A monk when he sings is more deeply penetrated by his understanding of the mysteries he proclaims than a layman can be, and this fact also has its effect on his delivery of the sacred melodies. As for the music itself, it is for the most part very simple in structure and shows a certain preference for recitative.

Greek Church music is quite different. Its tonality is foreign to our ears, but when one has become more accustomed to it, one notices the great diversity in its means of expression. Russian music often seems somewhat melancholy; Greek music, on the other hand, does justice to the whole range of emotions, but in an idiom that for Western Europeans and even for Russians sounds entirely foreign. The record that accompanies this book affords a possibility for comparing the two styles.

Dom Gregory Bainbridge, Chevetogne.

The Most Important Dates in the History of Athos

9th Century: The first records of the existence of hermits and small monastic settlements on Athos.

963 (961?) The foundation of the first large monastic community on Athos, the Great Lávra, by St. Athanásios.

971 The Emperor John Tsimiskis confirms the first Typikón (a sort of constitution) for the whole peninsula of Athos.

10th and 11th centuries: Most of the existing ruling monasteries are founded. A too rapid increase in the number of monks leads to a decay in discipline.

1045 The drafting of a second Typikón: Athos receives the title "Holy Mountain".

1169 Foundation of the first Russian ruling monastery.

1198 Building of the Serbian monastery of Chilandári.

15th century: Rise and expansion of the idiorhythmic system.

1430 Thessalonica and Athos come under Turkish rule.

1453 Sultan Mohammed II, the conqueror of Constantinople, confirms in a charter the autonomy of the peninsula of Athos within the Turkish Empire.

16th century: Rise of the Skití.

17th century: All twenty monasteries have been converted to the idiorhythmic rule. Decline of the monasticism of Athos.

18th century: Renewal of monasticism on the Holy Mountain. The number of the monks increases and the discipline improves.

1743 Foundation of the Athos Academy.

1783 The Patriarch Gabriel IV grants the Holy Mountain a new Typikón. The erection of the Ierá Kinótis.

1784 Eleven ruling monasteries begin a return to the cenobitic form of monasticism.

1821 Revolt of the Greeks against the Turkish domination, in which the monks take part. Athos is conquered, laid waste and occupied by 3000 Turkish soldiers.

1912 The Greek army frees the Holy Mountain from Turkish rule.

1924 In a general assembly the ruling monasteries evolve and approve the constitution valid today.

1926 The constitution is recognised and guaranteed by the Greek State.

1953 Foundation of the new School of Athos.

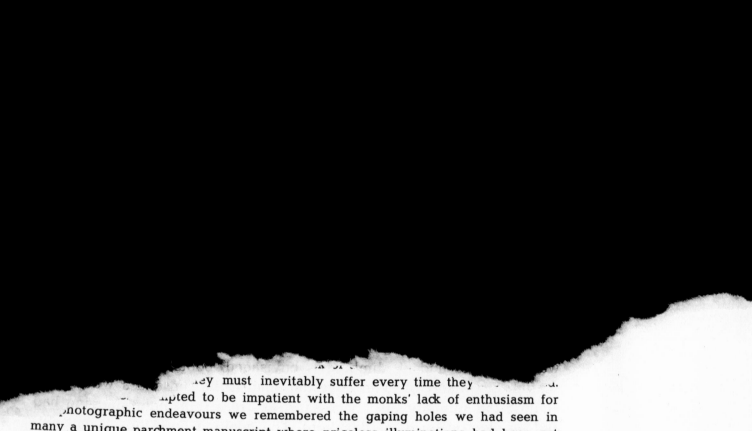

...ey must inevitably suffer every time they ....d.
....pted to be impatient with the monks' lack of enthusiasm for
photographic endeavours we remembered the gaping holes we had seen in many a unique parchment manuscript where priceless illuminations had been cut out with sharp knives, the shameful work of our predecessors, possibly photographers.

For these as well as for other reasons churches and chapels on Athos are kept closed except during services. Libraries and treasure chambers may be visited at certain times and by arrangement with the Guest Master or one of the senior monks. On these occasions photography is almost always forbidden, and the Librarian, or Sacristan in charge will make no exception to the rule. In their efforts not to offend the importunate photographer but determined not to relax the rule they sometimes argue vaguely that their monastery possesses no illuminated manuscripts or gold and silver ornaments worth photographing. In some houses the Librarian or Sacristan simply failed to turn up for an appointment, thus hoping to avoid further requests on our part that must be painfully turned down on his.

In some exceptional cases, based on reasons that can be proved to be of real importance, permission to photograph certain specific objects may be obtained from the Monastic Government at Karyés, or from the abbot of the monastery concerned. We ourselves received a most generous and comprehensive permission to take the photographs for this book which is being published in connection with the thousandth anniversary of Mount Athos. On our journeys we met scholars engaged in photographing unpublished ancient manuscripts in order to make them available for research.

For first class results the whole of one's equipment should be checked before leaving for Athos where nothing in the way of camera accessories, film or advice will be available. Different kinds of film should be tried out beforehand in order to test their sensitivity, and the electric cells of exposure metres should be checked and if necessary renewed, cells that have grown weak often being the cause of over-exposed pictures. A reliable flash apparatus, preferably with a

The Essentials of the Constitution of Athos

The juridical position of Athos has been laid down by a governmental decree of the Greek Republic of September 10th, 1926, by which the Greek State declares and makes binding in international law that "the peninsula of Athos constitutes an autonomous part of the Greek State, retaining full sovereignity over itself". All who at that date lived on Athos as monks and were accepted by the monasteries automatically became Greek citizens.

"The government of the Holy Mountain is exercised by the representatives of the twenty ruling monasteries, who form the Ierá Kinótis (the monastic parliament). The constitutional charter of the Holy Mountain regulates the details of governmental activity."

This constitution was carefully worked out by the monks themselves, taking into account a tradition one thousand years old, the foundational charters of individual monasteries, Imperial and Patriarchal Bulls and the enactments of Turkish Sultans. It was agreed and declared legal at a meeting of the General Assembly of the ruling monasteries on the 10th of May 1924 (according to the Julian calender).

The individual monasteries remain entirely independent as to the administration of their own property and the regulation of their internal affairs. Each of the twenty ruling monasteries elects one representative annually from among its monks to take part in the parliament that governs the community of the Holy Mountain. All twenty representatives are equal as to rights and duties and, according to an order of precedence laid down in the constitution, four of their number are named "Epistáte" and form the executive body of the Government. The Protepistátis, or Prótos, who is the head of the government, is chosen from among the four Epistáte. In practice his power is no greater than that of the other three Epistáte but he presides over the sessions of parliament, and other governmental activities are carried out under his presidency.

The monks of Athos acknowledge as their sole spiritual superior the Patriarch of Constantinople.

The Greek State is represented on the Holy Mountain by a civil governor who is served by a certain number of clerks and who has at his disposal a small corps of police and customs officers for the maintenance of public order on the peninsula.

No one who is not a Greek citizen by birth may become a monk of any monastery on Athos. Neither may he join a Skití or live there as a hermit.

Advice to Travellers to Athos

Before setting foot on the land of monks every visitor must have certain official documents and permissions without which the Athos passport cannot be issued to him at Karyés. Clergy of all denominations must a good two months before setting out on their journey obtain a special permit to visit Athos from the Patriarch of Constantinople and from the Foreign Office at Athens. Women are forbidden access to Mount Athos. This ruling is centuries' old and no exception can be made to it. All other travellers in possession of a valid passport can obtain, at Salonica, an authorisation good for a five day visit without any difficulty. Those who wish to remain longer on the peninsula must obtain a special permission from the Foreign Office at Athens. As this involves filling in questionnaires it is advisable to make one's application four to six weeks in advance.

When the prospective Athos visitor arrives at Salonica he should proceed first to the Government Buildings and there obtain, from the office of the Secretary General of the Greek Foreign Office, an entrance permit for Athos. Next he should visit the police station, which is situated on the outskirts of the city in the direction of the airport, where he will be issued with a certificate. Armed with these two documents he is then free to set out for Athos. The usual means of transport is a bus to Ierissós and it is advisable to book seats the day before departure at the bus terminal. It is opposite the Cathedral of St. Dimítrios.

When we made the trip, the bus for Ierissós left at eight o'clock in the morning. After three hours, a stop of one hour is made at Arnéa. Three hours later one reaches Ierissós and the end of the journey for that day. The traveller must spend the night at Ierissós and proceed early next morning, once again by bus, to Tripití, which is approximately two miles distant, and where he embarks for Dáphni on a boat that leaves at about seven o'clock, reaching Dáphni some three hours later. There, when he has gone through the Athos customs formalities, he is free to travel to Karyés, the seat of the Monastic Government and of all the administrative offices. Before setting out for Karyés, which is a three hour's climb from Dáphni, it is wise to eat something at the small restaurant in the port.

In order to complete all the necessary formalities on the first day it is essential to reach Karyés by four o'clock in the afternoon. First of all the visitor must present himself at the police station and hand over the certificate with which he was furnished by the police at Salonica. In exchange for this he receives a new document from the Athos police. This, together with the entrance permit obtained at the office of the Secretary General of the Foreign Office at Salonica, he takes to the Government Building where a monk issues the diamonitírion, or Athos passport, against a fee that varies according to the

we̶a̶t̶h̶e̶r̶ and, if climbing is envisaged, boots are essential. Some sort of head covering against the sun and a wrap against the rain are also necessary, as are a thin, light sleeping bag and an electric torch, or flashlight. The cooking on Athos is entirely based on olive oil that, as elsewhere on the Mediterranean, is not always refined, and does not invariably agree with everybody. A supply of food, in the lightest possible containers, is consequently a good investment.

While equipping oneself for the journey it is most important to keep in mind that only essentials should be packed and should fit in the rucksack that will be one's inseparable companion during the long hours of toiling along mountain roads and paths. Superfluous luggage can always be left behind at Salonica and picked up on one's return. The currency of Athos is the Greek drachma and money should be changed at Salonica, as no banking or exchange facilities exist on Athos.

The Essentials of the Constitution of Athos

The juridical position of Athos has been laid down by a governmental decree of the Greek Republic of September 10th, 1926, by which the Greek State declares and makes binding in international law that "the peninsula of Athos constitutes an autonomous part of the Greek State, retaining full sovereignity over itself". All who at that date lived on Athos as monks and were accepted by the monasteries automatically became Greek citizens.

"The government of the Holy Mountain is exercised by the representatives of the twenty ruling monasteries, who form the Ierá Kinótis (the monastic parliament). The constitutional charter of the Holy Mountain regulates the details of governmental activity."

This constitution was carefully worked out by the monks themselves, taking into account a tradition one thousand years old, the foundational charters of individual monasteries, Imperial and Patriarchal Bulls and the enactments of Turkish Sultans. It was agreed and declared legal at a meeting of the General Assembly of the ruling monasteries on the 10th of May 1924 (according to the Julian calender).

The individual monasteries remain entirely independent as to the administration of their own property and the regulation of their internal affairs. Each of the twenty ruling monasteries elects one representative annually from among its monks to take part in the parliament that governs the community of the Holy Mountain. All twenty representatives are equal as to rights and duties and, according to an order of precedence laid down in the constitution, four of their number are named "Epistáte" and form the executive body of the Government. The Protepistátis, or Prótos, who is the head of the government, is chosen from among the four Epistáte. In practice his power is no greater than that of the other three Epistáte but he presides over the sessions of parliament, and other governmental activities are carried out under his presidency.

The monks of Athos acknowledge as their sole spiritual superior the Patriarch of Constantinople.

The Greek State is represented on the Holy Mountain by a civil governor who is served by a certain number of clerks and who has at his disposal a small corps of police and customs officers for the maintenance of public order on the peninsula.

No one who is not a Greek citizen by birth may become a monk of any monastery on Athos. Neither may he join a Skití or live there as a hermit.

Advice to Travellers to Athos

Before setting foot on the land of monks every visitor must have certain official documents and permissions without which the Athos passport cannot be issued to him at Karyés. Clergy of all denominations must a good two months before setting out on their journey obtain a special permit to visit Athos from the Patriarch of Constantinople and from the Foreign Office at Athens. Women are forbidden access to Mount Athos. This ruling is centuries' old and no exception can be made to it. All other travellers in possession of a valid passport can obtain, at Salonica, an authorisation good for a five day visit without any difficulty. Those who wish to remain longer on the peninsula must obtain a special permission from the Foreign Office at Athens. As this involves filling in questionnaires it is advisable to make one's application four to six weeks in advance.

When the prospective Athos visitor arrives at Salonica he should proceed first to the Government Buildings and there obtain, from the office of the Secretary General of the Greek Foreign Office, an entrance permit for Athos. Next he should visit the police station, which is situated on the outskirts of the city in the direction of the airport, where he will be issued with a certificate. Armed with these two documents he is then free to set out for Athos. The usual means of transport is a bus to Ierissós and it is advisable to book seats the day before departure at the bus terminal. It is opposite the Cathedral of St. Dimítrios.

When we made the trip, the bus for Ierissós left at eight o'clock in the morning. After three hours, a stop of one hour is made at Arnéa. Three hours later one reaches Ierissós and the end of the journey for that day. The traveller must spend the night at Ierissós and proceed early next morning, once again by bus, to Tripití, which is approximately two miles distant, and where he embarks for Dáphni on a boat that leaves at about seven o'clock, reaching Dáphni some three hours later. There, when he has gone through the Athos customs formalities, he is free to travel to Karyés, the seat of the Monastic Government and of all the administrative offices. Before setting out for Karyés, which is a three hour's climb from Dáphni, it is wise to eat something at the small restaurant in the port.

In order to complete all the necessary formalities on the first day it is essential to reach Karyés by four o'clock in the afternoon. First of all the visitor must present himself at the police station and hand over the certificate with which he was furnished by the police at Salonica. In exchange for this he receives a new document from the Athos police. This, together with the entrance permit obtained at the office of the Secretary General of the Foreign Office at Salonica, he takes to the Government Building where a monk issues the diamonitírion, or Athos passport, against a fee that varies according to the visitor's business on the island. On receiving this document the visitor is entitled to travel throughout the peninsula and to be received at any of the monasteries.

Koutloumousíou monastery, a fifteen minutes' walk from Karyés, proves a hospitable place to spend one's first night on Athos. The Guest Master will be delighted to prepare a hot meal of tea, bread and vegetables for a weary guest. While no monastery charges anything for feeding or housing visitors, it must be remembered that they are not rich and the best way of helping towards one's board and lodging is to leave the Guest Master an envelope containing twenty or thirty drachmas.

It cannot be stressed too often that on entering Athos one steps into another world. All those conveniences and so-called necessities that are taken for granted in the world of men are left behind. There are no chemist shops or drug stores on Athos. The visitor will therefore be well advised to foresee the possibility of blisters, upset stomach, sunburn and insect bites, and provide himself with a compact, but complete medicine chest. Unless he rides a mule, the visitor will explore the unrivalled beauties of Athos on foot. Comfortable walking shoes and, if climbing is envisaged, boots, are therefore essential. Some sort of head covering against the sun and a waterproof against the rain are also necessary, as are a thin, light sleeping bag and an electric torch, or flashlight. The cooking on Athos is entirely based on olive oil that, as elsewhere on the Mediterranean, is not always refined, and does not invariably agree with everybody. A supply of food, in the lightest possible containers, is consequently a good investment.

While equipping oneself for the journey it is most important to keep in mind that only essentials should be packed and should fit in the rucksack that will be one's inseparable companion during the long hours of toiling along mountain roads and paths. Superfluous luggage can always be left behind at Salonica and picked up on one's return. The currency of Athos is the Greek drachma and money should be changed at Salonica, as no banking or exchange facilities exist on Athos.

Notes on Photography on Athos

Most visitors to Athos are equipped with a camera to record, either in black and white or in colour, the extraordinarily beautiful landscape of the island and the majesty of its unique architectural, artistic and religious tradition. It must always be remembered, however, that it is not a tourist land but essentially a religious one and therefore simply to photograph right and left from the very first moment would be a grave photographic error. The real Athos can only be discovered, and therefore photographed, by someone who approaches it reverently, with open eyes, mind, and heart.

The eager photographer should also remember the kind of impression he himself can make. Even in the outside world he tends to cut a brazen figure, tactless and impertinent unless he is careful. How much more careful must he be in this land of monks whose traditional hospitality is famous but who look with distrust and complete lack of sympathy on such worldly curiosity as is expressed by photographers, journalists, and historians of art, to say nothing of the apparently pointless photographic activity of tourists. Casually clicking cameras are a profanation of the monastic seclusion of their religious world, and the irreverent flashing of bulbs in the sacred precincts of their churches is all but intolerable to them. True reverence, understanding, and tact are therefore essential. More ambitious photographers who aspire to record ancient charters, fragments of Holy Scripture, priceless illuminated manuscripts, and icons, must also remember that the monks have laboured for centuries, often at the risk of their lives, to preserve such treasures intact, and that they must inevitably suffer every time they are handled. If ever we were tempted to be impatient with the monks' lack of enthusiasm for our photographic endeavours we remembered the gaping holes we had seen in many a unique parchment manuscript where priceless illuminations had been cut out with sharp knives, the shameful work of our predecessors, possibly photographers.

For these as well as for other reasons churches and chapels on Athos are kept closed except during services. Libraries and treasure chambers may be visited at certain times and by arrangement with the Guest Master or one of the senior monks. On these occasions photography is almost always forbidden, and the Librarian, or Sacristan in charge will make no exception to the rule. In their efforts not to offend the importunate photographer but determined not to relax the rule they sometimes argue vaguely that their monastery possesses no illuminated manuscripts or gold and silver ornaments worth photographing. In some houses the Librarian or Sacristan simply failed to turn up for an appointment, thus hoping to avoid further requests on our part that must be painfully turned down on his.

In some exceptional cases, based on reasons that can be proved to be of real importance, permission to photograph certain specific objects may be obtained from the Monastic Government at Karyés, or from the abbot of the monastery concerned. We ourselves received a most generous and comprehensive permission to take the photographs for this book which is being published in connection with the thousandth anniversary of Mount Athos. On our journeys we met scholars engaged in photographing unpublished ancient manuscripts in order to make them available for research.

For first class results the whole of one's equipment should be checked before leaving for Athos where nothing in the way of camera accessories, film or advice will be available. Different kinds of film should be tried out beforehand in order to test their sensitivity, and the electric cells of exposure metres should be checked and if necessary renewed, cells that have grown weak often being the cause of over-exposed pictures. A reliable flash apparatus, preferably with a second lamp, is essential for the interior of churches and monasteries or for portraits and groups in rooms where daylight is usually insufficient. Finally it must not be forgotten that on Athos electricity does not exist. Electric lamps and spotlights are therefore useless, nor can batteries be recharged. Neither can a car battery be resorted to in an emergency since cars are not allowed on the island. The state of the roads makes driving impossible. Whoever drives from Salonica to Athos must leave his car at Ierissós and pick it up on the way back.

Photographic and Technical data:

The photographs in this book were taken with Leica III f, Leica III g and Linhof-Technika 6×9.

Leica lenses: Summaron 2.8 cm. Summaron 3.5 cm. Elmar 5 cm. Summicron 5 cm. Summarex 8.5 cm. Elmar 9 cm. Hektor 13.5 cm. Telyt 20 cm. Kilfitt: Tele-Kilar 30 cm.

Linhof-Technika lenses: Angulon 1:6.8/65 cm. Xenar 1:3.5/105 cm. Tele-Xenar 1:5.5/180 cm.

Flash apparatus: Braun-Hobby and battery; Mannesmann, Multiblitz-Press and eight accumulator batteries.

Exposure meters: Bertram-München, Chronos and Electro-Bewi.

All seven thousand photographs were taken exclusively on AGFA-Film: Agfacolor CUT 18, CNT 17, Isopan 17/10 and 21/10 Din.

Books on Athos, Icons and Eastern Spirituality

Amand de Mendieta, Emmanuel, *La presqu'île des Caloyers, le Mont Athos*, Bruges, Desclée de Brouwer, 1955, x-388 pp.

Brockhaus, Heinrich, *Die Kunst in den Athos-Klöstern*, 2nd edn., Leipzig, Brockhaus, 1924, xll-335 pp.

Byron, Robert, *The Station, Athos: Treasures and Men*, 2nd. edn., London, John Lehmann, 1949, 263 pp.

Cavarnos, Constantine, *Anchored in God*, Athens, "Astir", 1959, 230 pp.

Dawkins, R. M., *The Monks of Athos*, London, G. Allen and Unwin, 1936, 408 pp.

Dionysius of Furna, *Hermeneia* (Guide to Painters) trans. P. Durand, in Didron, A-N., *Manuel d'Iconographie Chrétienne Grecque et Latine*, Paris, Impr. Royale, 1845, xlviii-483 pp. (English trans., with notes abridged, in Didron and Stokes, *Christian Iconography*, II, London, G. Bell, 1886, pp. 265-399.

Dölger, Franz (ed.), *Mönchsland Athos*, Munich, Bruckmann, 1943, 303 pp.

Dölger, Franz, *Aus den Schatzkammern des Heiligen Berges*, 2 vols., Munich, Bruckmann, 1948, 363 + 128 pp.

Felicetti-Liebenfels, Walter, *Geschichte der byzantinischen Ikonenmalerei*, Olten-Lausanne, Urs Graf Verlag, 1956, 134 pp. and 136 pl.

Hasluck, F. W., *Athos and its Monasteries*, London, Kegan Paul. etc. — New York E. P. Dutton, 1924, xll-214 pp.

Kadloubovsky, E. and Palmer, G. E. H., *Writings from the Philokalia on Prayer of the Heart* (trans. from the Russian), London, Faber & Faber, 1951, 420 pp.

Loch, Sydney, *Athos, the Holy Mountain*, London, Lutterworth, 1957, 264 pp.

Lossky, Vladimir, *The Mystical Theology of the Eastern Church*, London, J. Clarke, 1957, 252 pp.

Meyendorff, Jean, *Introduction à l'étude de Grégoire Palamas*, Paris, Seuil, 1959, 432 pp.

Millet, Gabriel, *Monuments de l'Athos*, I, Les Peintures, Paris, E. Leroux, 1927, 75 pp. (264 pl.).

Monk of the Eastern Church, *Orthodox Spirituality*, London, S. P. C. K. 1957, xiv-104 pp.

Idem, *La Prière de Jésus*, 3rd edn., Chevetogne, 1959.

Idem, *Jesus: Simples regards sur le Sauveur*, Chevetogne, 1960, 196 pp.

Sherrard, Philip, *Athos, Mountain of Silence*, London, Oxford University Press, to appear early in 1960.

Further bibliography in Amand de Mendieta (1955) and Dölger, *Mönchsland Athos*, 1943.

Notes

1. The chapters, "The Lávra, First of the Ruling Monasteries"; "Vatopédi, the Academy, and the New School of Athos"; "The Twenty Ruling Monasteries"; "The Katholikón" and "Easter" were written by Dom Ludger Bernhard; the other chapters by the author.

2. Translation of the diamonitírion, page 47:

The diamonitírion, or passport reproduced here, which is, as usual, written in the form of a letter of recommendation "To our twenty holy and most venerable Monasteries of the Holy Mountain of Athos", departs from the usual pattern as regards its contents. It states that the persons "who carry with them this letter have received a special, official, comprehensive permission from the Monastic Government, by whom they have been invited to take definitive photographs of the most beautiful Byzantine and post-Byzantine artistic and historical monuments and objects (icons, illuminated manuscripts, etc.), to be used in the publication of books on the Holy Mountain and of souvenir books for visitors to Athos. We recommend them most especially therefore to your well-Beloved Reverence and ask you, as brothers, that they be granted every facility and permission for their work as well as your well known and traditional hospitality. With brotherly greetings: The Provost of the Monastic Government of the Holy Mountain of Athos". There follow the signatures of the Prótos and of the Epistáte.

3. The Great Schíma, page 132. The Greek text and its translation. A song of praise to the Holy Cross:

Ἰησοῦς Χριστὸς ΝιϰᾶΙ
Τετιμημένον Τρόπαιον Δαιμόνων Φρίϰη
Ῥητοριϰωτέρα Ῥημάτων Δαϰρύων Ῥοή
Χριστὸς Χριστιανοῖς Χαρίζεται Χάριν
Θεὸς Ἡγίασε Σταυροῦ Ξύλον
Ἑωσφόρος Ἔπεσεν Εὑρήϰαμεν Ἐδέμ
Φῶς Χριστοῦ Φαίνει Πᾶσι
Δύναμις Μοναχοῦ
Τόπος Κρανίου Παράδεισος Γέγονεν

Jesus Christ is victorius.
The venerated sign of victory, the Terror of the demons,
Well of tears, more eloquent than all words.
Christ grants grace to Christians!
God hallowed the wood of the Cross,
Lucifer is fallen; we have found the garden of Eden!
The light of Christ shines before all men,
Golgotha, the place of the skull has become Paradise.

4. The Slavonic chants were recorded in the monastery of Chevetogne, in Belgium, where for many years the same melodies as in the Russian monastery of St. Pandeleímon on Athos have been sung. At St. Pandeleímon Church Slavonic chant is hardly possible any longer because of the lack of adequate voices. At the turn of the century two thousand monks lived there but since the end of the First World War Russians have been forbidden to enter Athos monasteries and the number of monks at St. Pandeleímon has dwindled to about fifty, most of whom are over seventy years of age.

5. The celebration of the thousandth anniversary of Athos was originally planned for early in 1961, but the final date has not yet been fixed. There are two traditions on Athos as to the foundation of the first monastery, the Lávra, by St. Athanásios. One holds that it took place in 961, the other in 963. It seems likely that the celebration will be postponed until 1963.

6. The publishers of the anniversary edition are bringing out editions (complete with record) in German, French, and Greek. Editions in other languages will follow.

Contents of the Record

Side 1.

1. Bells (festal chimes).
2. Beating of the Símandron (to announce the Office).
3. The Great Litany (excerpt): Deacon and Choir.

Mírom Góspodu pomólimsya. Góspodi pomílui.

In peace let us pray to the Lord. Lord have mercy.

For the peace that cometh from above and the salvation of our souls, let us pray to the Lord.

For the peace of the whole world, for the tranquillity of the holy Churches of God and for the unity of all men, let us pray to the Lord.

For this holy house and all who enter it with faith, reverence, and the fear of God, let us pray to the Lord. (...)

For those at sea, for travellers, for the sick, the suffering, prisoners, and for their salvation, let us pray to the Lord.

For our deliverance from all affliction, wrath, and need, let us pray to the Lord.

Making memory of our all-holy, immaculate, most blessed, and glorious Lady, the Mother of God and ever Virgin Mary together with all the saints, let us commend ourselves, one another, and our whole life to Christ our God. To Thee, O Lord.

For to Thee is due all glory, honour and worship, Father, Son, and Holy Ghost, now and for ever and to ages unending. Amen.

4. Vesper psalm with Alleluia refrain.

Blazhén muzh, allilúia.

Blessed is the man, alleluia, who walketh not in the counsels of the ungodly, alleluia, alleluia, alleluia. For the Lord knoweth the way of the righteous; and the way of the ungodly shall come to nought, alleluia, alleluia, alleluia. Serve ye the Lord in fear, and rejoice before Him in trembling, alleluia, alleluia, alleluia. Arise, Lord, save me, O Thou, my God, alleluia, alleluia, alleluia. Alleluia, alleluia, alleluia, glory be to Thee, O God (three times).

5. Greek Solo.

Christós anésti ek nekrón.

Christ is risen from among the dead, trampling on death by His death and granting life to those in the tomb.

Glory be to the Father, and to the Son, and to the Holy Ghost; now and for ever and to ages unending, Amen.

Side 2.

1. The Cherubic Hymn.

Ishe Kheruvímy táyno obrazúyushche.

Putting on the mystic likeness of the Cherubim and singing to the life-giving Trinity the thrice-holy hymn, let us now forgo all worldly cares, (Amen) that we may welcome the King of all escorted by invisible companies of angels, alleluia, alleluia, alleluia.

2. Hymn to the Blessed Virgin (the evening, after Compline).

Pod tvoyú mílost pribegáyem, Bogoróditse Dévo.

We fly for help to thy mercy, Virgin Mother of God, despise not the prayers we make in our afflictions, but deliver us from all our ills, thou alone all pure and blessed Maid. All-holy Mother of God, save us.

NOTE ON SPELLING AND PRONUNCIATION

With the exception of a very few proper names, all Greek words in the present book are written in such a way as to enable the reader to pronounce them as they are pronounced today in Greece. Many of them may seem a little strange, but our intention being to open a door of understanding between Western European culture and Greece, this has seemed to us a modest but useful contribution to this task.

In our system of transcription every word carries a tonic accent.

ch = German *ch* in *machen* or *ich*
th = English *th* in *thin*
i = English *ee* in *see*
e = English *e* in *set*
y = English *y* in *yes*

Note therefore that *Skití* would rhyme with *tea-leaf* and *Skíte* (the plural) with *tea-set*.

Imprimi potest, Maria Laach, 15. 8. 1959
✝ Basilius Ebel, Abt

Imprimatur, Freiburg i. Br., 1. 9. 1959
Föhr, Generalvikar

INDEX